JUDAISM AND CHRISTIANITY

VOL. III

LAW AND RELIGION

JUDAISM AND CHRISTIANITY

VOLUME III
LAW AND RELIGION

Essays by

J. MURPHY, T. FISH, H. WHEELER ROBINSON,
E. ROBERTSON, R. TRAVERS HERFORD, T. W.
MANSON, H. A. R. GIBB, E. I. J. ROSENTHAL,
V. McNABB

*With a Foreword by WILLIAM TEMPLE,
ARCHBISHOP OF YORK,
and an Afterword by HERBERT M. J. LOEWE,
Reader in Rabbinics in the University of Cambridge*

Edited by

ERWIN I. J. ROSENTHAL

LONDON
THE SHELDON PRESS
NORTHUMBERLAND AVENUE, W.C. 2
NEW YORK: THE MACMILLAN COMPANY

First published *1938*

Made in Great Britain

FOREWORD

THIS volume serves—and serves admirably—a double purpose. First it carries further the work of this series, helping modern English people to appreciate their double debt to Judaism and to Christianity, and so the more readily, as one hopes, to regard with sympathy and friendliness the Jewish people who now so urgently need both. Secondly the book helps to clarify, by tracing their history, some elements in the idea of Law, a grasp of which is again becoming of vital importance to civilization. The former purpose is quite as relevant to contemporary problems as the latter ; but it is in some respects a special instance of the latter, and anyhow it is only of this that I have any qualification to speak.

Until very recent times most people were content to take the idea of Law for granted. Its importance to social and therefore also to individual well-being was obvious. Its relation to Justice on the one hand, and to Sovereignty on the other was less obvious ; but there was general agreement that while the Sovereign (however constituted) was the source and guarantor of Law, there was an obligation upon the Sovereign to make the Law just so far as might be. Again, while few would be ready to offer a definition of Justice—and the more they had reflected upon it, the less ready would they be—there was a general agreement that it was closely related to personality,

and that a person could have just rights against the
state of which he was a citizen.

Now this fundamental doctrine is challenged. On
no such theory of justice can the treatment of the Jews
in Germany and Austria be upheld or even tolerated.
And indeed that whole theory of justice is avowedly
abandoned alike in Germany and in Russia. Justice,
we are told by official spokesmen of both those
countries, is the interest of the state. This will
usually, though not necessarily, cover the maintenance
of equity between individual citizens, but their claim
to this is not derived from their *status* as human beings,
but from the interest of the state in possessing con-
tented and loyal citizens. In some cases, as that of
the Jews in Germany, it is held that their presence in
the community is contrary to the interest of the
community—which is therefore acting justly when it
expropriates them, or (to use the phrase preferred in
Russia) " liquidates " them.

If we are to be safe against infection from this
heresy, we must know what are the real roots of
Law as we understand it and (in the main) enjoy it.
We then find that historically it has two roots—in the
Roman Law which is traceable to the Stoics, and in
the Jewish Law drawn from the Old Testament.

The Christian tradition has been more influenced
by the Roman source than has the Jewish ; and it is
very wholesome for us to consider how far this influence of Roman and Stoic conceptions should be
allowed to prevail. For while that tradition treats
men as individuals, " each counting for one and none
for more than one," it treats individuals rather as
specimens of a genus than as persons. For all personal relations are special ; none is merely general.

Our penal system increasingly recognizes this. No
man is merely a criminal ; and if the state treats him
as a criminal and nothing else it makes a mistake and
commits an injustice. If a man on some occasion
stole a jewel, he is a thief and must be treated as a
thief ; but he is not only a thief, and must be treated
with regard to his other qualities also.

But it would be easy to press this emphasis on the
concrete uniqueness of every person to a point where
it involves chaos. To cut short an argument which
might easily extend to the length of one of the following lectures, it is precisely the special characteristic
of the Jewish tradition which supplies the solution.
For in this tradition, behind all legalist enactments or
precepts is the apprehension of God as the Living
God who created man in His own image, and whose
personal care for every man is the spring of the Law
which he makes for men.

Law and Freedom are closely allied, as every
political philosophy recognizes. But Law and Freedom, as we have learnt to value them, are alike
products of faith in God as alone absolute, and in
His fatherly care for men, each of whom has *status*
and value as a child of God which are prior to his
status and value as a citizen of any state or as a member
of any race. This belief is alone able to support in
harmony the two elements of universality and
uniqueness in the social relationships which Law
exists to regulate.

WILLIAM EBOR :

PREFACE

THIS third volume of *Judaism and Christianity* has grown out of the second. As the result of a correspondence between its editor, Mr. H. Loewe, and the present editor, it was suggested that " the relation between Law and Religion " should be dealt with in a course of lectures under the auspices of the Semitics Department of this University. Professor E. Robertson, the head of the Semitics Department, readily gave his permission and encouragement, and the Extra-Mural Department co-operated.

The volume follows the lines of its predecessors : impartial presentation of a subject common to Judaism and Christianity. It differs from its predecessors in that one central theme has been chosen. It was felt that to concentrate on one question would permit of an historical treatment of the subject.

The tradition of the Hebrews asserts two things of the Law : (i) What it was in itself : a guide to good life according to the mind of God ; a guide which is all-embracing, as is religion whence it sprang. (ii) Its source : God who *revealed* it.

The first point will be abundantly clear from the lectures which deal with the Torah in its various stages in the various ages. The second point is not so obvious from the lectures. Nowhere is the Hebrew tradition denied, yet it cannot be said that the historical truth of that tradition is assumed by all in

the sense in which Hebrew tradition understands
" revelation " of the Torah.

As was fitting, the majority of the lectures dealt
with the Torah throughout the Old Testament, in
Pharisaism, in the New Testament, in mediæval
Jewish and Christian thought. Others were added
as collateral and in some respects relevant matter :
the first on the religious origins of Law ; the second
on the Law as revealed amongst the Babylonians and
Assyrians. Two others deal with Law amongst peoples
having roots in Hebrew tradition : the Samaritans
who claim a monopoly of the Pentateuchal Torah,
and the peoples of Islam whose prophet is " the seal
of the prophets." The lectures might have been
more comprehensive ; Egypt would have been added
had that been possible, and present-day thought on
Torah amongst Jews and Gentiles would have provided interesting matter. Also a paper on the attitude
of modern states to the laws of the Torah would have
been most valuable. But the lectures here printed
are enough for one volume and contain matter which
may suggest to others topics for further discussion.

It remains to express my warm thanks to all the
contributors for their help in giving the papers and
in correspondence ; to the Archbishop of York for
his Foreword ; to Mr. H. Loewe for generous encouragement and advice throughout ; to Professor
Robertson in especial, who encouraged the project
and negotiated the inception and presided over
the several meetings ; to Mr. Pilkington Turner, the
head of the Extra-Mural Department, which adopted
the course and advertised it ; to the Council of
the University for supplying any funds needed to
meet the expenses of the course ; to the Rev. R. H.

Hughes, B.A., B.D., for compiling the Index ; and to
Dr. T. Fish, who has given me valuable help in
preparing this volume for the press.

The contributors wish to thank the printers for their
exceptional care and skill in dealing with technical
material.

E. ROSENTHAL.

MANCHESTER UNIVERSITY,
      SEMITICS DEPARTMENT.

CONTENTS

I

PRIMITIVE ORIGINS OF LAW IN RELATION TO RELIGION

BY

J. MURPHY

I

PRIMITIVE ORIGINS OF LAW IN RELATION TO RELIGION

To speak of " origins " and especially of "*primitive*" origins in relation to any subject implies that it has had a history ; that it has been and is a living and developing thing. Like everything that lives on this earth, Law has grown, as it were, from childhood to maturity ; and in order to understand it in the present, and in some measure to foresee its future, it is valuable and indeed necessary to see it grow, to trace its evolution from its most distant past. Lord Macmillan in his recent suggestive volume of essays says, speaking of the lawyer, " The system of rules and principles which he is daily called upon to apply is in large measure an inheritance from the past. It has been slowly built up during centuries of development and its sources are often to be found in the very beginnings of history. . . . A knowledge of the embryology of legal principles is essential to the understanding of them in their present developed form." [1] How true this is may become evident if we glance at a famous definition of Law which is really a description of its nature as understood in civilized states of the present day. It is the often quoted pronouncement of Mr. Justice Cardozo : " A principle or rule of

[1] Lord Macmillan, *Law and Other Things*, p. 123 (Cambridge, 1937).

conduct so established as to justify a prediction with reasonable certainty that it will be enforced by the courts if its authority is challenged, is a principle or rule of law." [1] There are indeed rules of conduct at all stages of the evolution of human society ; and the most primitive savages known to us have their initiations for their youth in which they are taught rules of conduct which are essentially the laws of the tribe ; but these are not so general or abstract as principles, which the primitive mind neither grasps nor formulates easily, but are rather statements of concrete, individual things they must not do. Further, there are no courts in our sense of the word with machinery for the enforcement of the law in the simpler societies. At times in the more organized tribes a few of the elders or headmen may pronounce upon a case and even fix a penalty ; but in most instances the redress is left either to the private vengeance of the injured man or his clan, or more frequently to the censure of public opinion to which the tribal savage is extremely sensitive, or more powerfully still to the mystical penalties of disease, misfortune or death which are believed to follow breaches of taboos or other offences against the unseen powers. This brief comparison of law as defined in civilized society to-day with the rules of conduct and the practical application of them in savage communities, gives a glimpse of the difference between them, and at the same time shows how the study of the attempts of primitive man to bring order and stability into his social relations does throw light upon the complex legal systems under which we live to-day, and which are actually de-

[1] Huntington Cairns, *Law and the Social Sciences*, pp. 12–13 (London, 1935).

veloped forms taken in the course of time by those primitive endeavours of ancient peoples.

This is the more interesting and important because, as we shall find illustrated more fully in our later survey of early history, there are curious survivals in modern legal theory and practice of the primitive ideas and customs of our forefathers. I may give but one illustration at the moment. It concerns the close relation between law and religion in their primitive forms. It is a characteristic of religious formulæ, and still more of the magico-religious spells and charms which preceded them in early society, that intense importance is attached to the pronouncement of the exact words, so that the slightest change would destroy the efficacy. W. A. Robson in his book, *Civilisation and the Growth of Law*, remarks on this feature in Roman Law in connexion with the point of the great influence of the priests and the religious ritual upon the early written law, such as the famous Twelve Tables. He gives an illustration as given by Gaius. " If, he said, you sued by *Legis Actio* for injury to your vines, and called them vines, you would fail in your claim, because the text of the Twelve Tables spoke only of trees." He adds that "A similar rigidity descended upon the old Teutonic Law. According to the Malberg Gloss, which contains a collection of ancient legal formulas, if a man sued for a bull, his action would fail if he described him as a bull. The animal had to be designated by the ancient juridical name of ' leader of the herd,' just as a goat had to be called the ' browser upon leeks ' and the forefinger of the hand the ' arrow-finger.' " [1] Lord Macmillan makes the same point, observing

[1] *Civilisation and the Growth of Law* (Macmillan), p. 71.

that " in English law the requirements of formalism were originally peculiarly stringent and there were many words of style which Maitland described as ' sacramental phrases.' The slightest slip in the use of the covenanted words was fatal." He tells that "so lately as 1901 an English judge was constrained to decide that a title to land was defective because a conveyance was expressed to be ' in fee ' instead of ' in fee simple,' although he was in no doubt as to what the parties intended. I have no doubt," he adds, " that in attributing a special solemnity to certain written or spoken words the law has been influenced by the primitive belief in the potency of spells and incantations." [1]

While there are survivals of the primitive even in our most modern legal systems, such as the stress on the letter of the law just mentioned, there is, naturally, more knowledge to be gained about the origins of law from a consideration of its earliest forms, which are to be found in the so-called Codes of the ancient civilizations. A recent book on Primitive Law by Mr. A. C. Diamond gives an account of these early collections of laws, of which the most ancient is the Code of Hammurabi,[2] which was discovered engraved upon a pillar of black diorite in 1902, and is dated to about the same number of centuries before the Christian era, about 1900 B.C. This, because of its early origin, is the most illuminating of all. Valuable because of the light they add to the Hammurabi document are certain Assyrian fragments, which have the special interest of revealing what is known from

[1] *Law and Other Things*, p. 73.
[2] [The Code of Hammurabi, in relation to Religion and Revelation, is dealt with in the next paper by Dr. Fish.—ED.]

other sources, namely, a savage cruelty in their penalties, in the form of mutilations, which is characteristic of the Assyrians in their days of power. There is also a Hittite Code, produced by that probably Aryan people in the fourteenth century B.C., but of a more primitive type than the laws of Hammurabi. There is the Hebrew Code in the narrow sense in which Mr. Diamond understands it, as covering the Book of the Covenant (Exodus xxi. 2 to xxii. 17) [1] ; and the later editions of the Torah, with its mingling of civil legislation, ritual ordinances, and moral and religious teaching. There are other codes or collections of laws which the author of *Primitive Law* employs as sources for his investigation, which belong to a much later time than those just mentioned, such as the early Roman collection of the Twelve Tables, dated about 194 B.C., the Code of Manu, the Indian compilation belonging to near the beginning of the Christian era, and the Anglo-Saxon Laws, particularly the code ascribed to Æthelberht, which are not earlier than the sixth or seventh century A.D. It is right that these later collections should be set for comparison beside the much more ancient laws, because they originate in a state of society closely similar to that in which the codes of the ancient peoples were compiled, namely, a stage in their history at which tribes not long emerged from barbarism were settling into states with a certain degree of civilized life. It was a time when unorganized customs, taboos and other rules of the tribe, had been thrown into confusion by migrations and other new conditions of life, and when it seemed opportune to various authoritative men to introduce

---

[1] [This part is singled out for its form in the Conditional.—ED.]

order by supplying, with the permanence of the written word, rules for the social conduct of the people which are rudimentary but true laws as judged by modern standards. It is a salient mark of their primitive character that these compilations are not codes in the modern sense, or as understood by lawyers of recent times, because they are not unified or organized under general principles which apply to many separate cases and situations, but are collections of rules for dealing with specific cases which may and do actually arise.

This distinction corresponds to a difference which we draw here between two types of mind, one of which we shall call the primitive and the other the civilized type. They are not absolutely different from each other, as the distinguished French writer M. Lévy-Bruhl has maintained ; [1] and the civilized develops out of the primitive—which he would deny ; [2] but one of the marked differences between them is this, that while, on the one hand, the civilized mind is capable of conceptual and abstract thought and thus of gathering many particulars under one general principle, or of making one law which applies to a great many similar situations, the primitive type of mind is atomistic, because the co-ordinative power of the mind is undeveloped. This means that, like the reflexes of instinct in the animal, and like the immediate response of action to perception in the undeveloped intelligence, the primitive human mind adjusts itself to each situation separately, and if it makes rules for the control of conduct, lays down a

[1] L. Lévy-Bruhl, *Les Fonctions mentales dans les sociétés inférieures*, p. 454 (Paris).
[2] *Ibid.*, p. 18.   Cf. *La Mentalité primitive*, pp. 15–16.

separate rule for each situation as it is imagined to arise. The early codes and their laws are thus intermediate between the primitive and the civilized products of intelligence, in that they are, on the one hand, the result of co-ordinative and conceptual thought in a simple form bringing together into one code, issued under one authority, a number of rules which are available for the community in an accessible form ; while, on the other hand, they retain the primitive, atomistic character of meeting each particular demand for guidance or judgment in its own particular way.

These early systems of law thus like Janus have two faces, one looking toward the more primitive age with its rules for adjusting social relations within the community, and the other toward the later times of civilized history with their complex legal systems and institutions. In order, then, to come yet nearer to the primitive beginnings it is natural to betake ourselves to the earlier forms of society which preceded the ancient civilizations, and out of which they were formed As a preliminary to this, however, it will be well to consider how these civilizations themselves originated. All of those societies which gave rise to the early codes of law, the Mesopotamian or Assyro-Babylonian, the Hittite, the Hebrew, the Greek and the early Roman, display certain characteristics in common, which also differentiate them from the more primitive social groups such as the tribe and the yet simpler clan. All of them, for instance, are based upon agriculture, farming and cattle-rearing ; they have cities and towns which are the nerve-centres of their polity ; their religions are all of a theistic pattern, that is, they worship gods who are conceived as personal more or less distinctly ; and at the same time, as a consequence of the varied demands and opportunities for personal initiative in thought, in work and art, there is a much higher degree of individuality in the ordinary population, and especially among the leisured class, than there is in the simpler societies, such as the tribal groups of the present day. There are two striking results of these conditions and characteristics of the ancient civilizations. One of them is that, as I have already hinted, there appears in them what is substantially a new type of mind. It may be called the Civilized Mind, because it remains to the present hour the way of thinking which marks the civilized man at his highest, and because it can be clearly distinguished from the typical mind of the primitive or the savage. Its distinctive qualities are the power of conceptual and abstract thought, the capacity for ethical judgment, and a new consciousness of individuality. The first took the place of the mainly perceptual consciousness issuing usually in semi-instinctive action in the form of obedience to some taboo or customary rite, characteristic of the primitive or tribal mind ; the second substituted for concrete responses to the authority of custom ideas of right and wrong, and even of sin and righteousness ; and the third made the tribesman, as the citizen of a large community and even of a world-empire, more of a personality. The religion of this type of mind undergoes a corresponding change from the spirit-worship of Animism, common at the tribal stage, to worship of gods, that is, personal deities in a polytheism in which there are certain tendencies to monotheism.

The second result issuing from the nature of the

early civilizations, and in particular from the development of the civilized type of mind, is seen in the
astonishing phenomenon which marks the last millennium before the Christian era, namely, the brilliant
constellation of prophetic men, teachers of religion,
morals and philosophy, who are clustered strikingly
in history from the eighth to the fifth or fourth
century B.C., but may be extended backwards in more
scattered numbers towards 1500 B.C. or even 2000 B.C.
Within the narrower sector from the eighth century
to the fourth, there are the great prophets of Israel,
the Buddha and the early philosopher-mystics of
Hinduism in India, the group of remarkable thinkers
around Confucius in China, and the mighty dramatists
and philosophers of Greece. A century or two earlier
came Zoroaster, the Aryan apostle of an early
monotheism ; in the fourteenth century Akhenaten,
the abstract thinker and teacher of an almost pure
monotheism in concrete-minded Egypt ; and if
Abraham and Moses are to be included among those
who wrought creatively upon the religion and law of
Israel, as recent evidence seems to confirm, the
prophetic horizon, as we may call it, must be a still
wider circle. The time element is not supremely
important, for genius takes ages in its stride ; but
what concerns us at the moment is the fact that the
conditions which made these prophets and teachers
possible were first provided in these early civilizations,
and that the civilized mind found its natural and yet
miraculous blossoming in these great thinkers and
founders of religious and moral systems.

There also emerge from the foregoing historical
sketch two important questions which it is convenient
to notice at this point. They have reference to the

relation of these creative minds of the prophetic horizon to the idea of a divine revelation, on the one hand, and to the ancient codes of law, on the other. It is indeed with the prophets and founders of religions that the conception of revelation originates ; for it is they who almost invariably declare that the truth which has come to them is a revelation of and from the Divine ; and the first question is what meaning is to be given or what reality can be ascribed to that revelation. The answer to that question depends upon the philosophic or religious standpoint which one takes ; and we shall postpone it to its place in our summary final discussion of the connexion between revelation and the origins of law. The second question arises from the fact that the origin of law in its true form as distinct from custom is often attributed in early history to these prophetic individuals, and that the codes, the first attempts to systematize it, are ascribed to their creative minds. It is a matter of some significance that this is not true. The early codes are little more than a setting together of rules already existing for dealing with particular occurrences and adding a few of the same nature ; and this can be done, and is done, by quite second-rate minds. The prophets, moral teachers, and founders of religions have a different function. They lay down great religious conceptions and supreme ethical principles ; and at times they are themselves striking exemplars of ideal conduct created by an inner law—by all of which things innumerable cases may be met, and existing law itself be judged, and if necessary be changed to a higher law. It is, moreover, the all but invariable characteristic of these thinkers to claim a vocation, and to ascribe the words they speak and the

new laws they bring—not as codes but as principles—
to a Divine Being whose will they express, in other
words, to a Divine revelation.

Dr. Gordon Childe has described the change which
produced the ancient civilizations from Egypt to
China, including Mesopotamia and the Indus cities,
in a brilliant generalization, as the result of two great
revolutions, namely, " the change from a food-
gathering to a food-producing economy, and the
establishment of urban civilization based upon in-
dustry and commerce." [1] We shall not enter into the
detail of his description, but may repeat its most
striking feature, viz. the emergence of a new type of
mind, the civilized as contrasted with the primitive
or (which is somewhat different) the tribal mind.
It might also be described as the deliverance of man
from the kingdom of custom into the kingdom of law.
In neither case is it advisable to exaggerate the
difference. It is, for instance, an over-emphasis for
M. Lévy-Bruhl to maintain that the primitive men-
tality is absolutely different from the civilized, that
the one, for example, is "prelogical," while the other is
" logical." It is the same machine that is used, but in
the one case, the operator is a learner and makes innumerable blunders, while in the other, reason is used
not infallibly but with skill and far less numerous mistakes. Similarly, one agrees that Professor Malinowski,
who has deservedly so great authority on this subject,
is right in criticizing the fancy picture of tribal man
drawn by some modern anthropologists, which portrayed him as an automaton moved only by custom,
the bond slave of tribal rules, without any initiative

[1] V. Gordon Childe, *New Light on the Most Ancient East*, p. 283
(London, 1934).

or personality of his own. Yet we shall not understand the intrusions of the primitive into our own
minds, or reversions in modern society to tribalism in
thought and practice, or the lingering vestiges of
ancient savagery which persist in law and punishment,
if we do not realize at once the touch of nature, of
the ancient, instinctive animal nature which makes
us akin to the primitive, and the powerful fears of
tribalism with their trust in solidarity for salvation
still crouching at the very door of the mind, and at
the same time how far, ideally at least, we have passed
beyond these.

1. *The Primitive in Early Law*

We may now turn to some examples of the contrast
between the primitive and the civilized type of mind,
and to observe these both in modern survivals and in
the ancient codes of law which are nearest to the
primitive.

The most primitive human being is nearest to the
animal from which he has sprung or been created.
Like the animal he acts very largely upon instinctive
impulse; and the end or terminus of such an impulse is
an action. Action under the influence of excitement
or emotion such as fear tends to be violent ; and the
unconscious impulse among the stronger animals, and
in man when he has no time or is too angry to think,
is to kill the living cause of the danger or annoyance.
The knock-out blow, putting the living machine out
of action, is safest to unthinking instinct. That is why
the death penalty is so frequent in primitive retaliation and in the earliest laws. An Australian aborigine
would kill his wife instantly if she stepped over him

as he lay on the ground. This expressed his panic-fear of the mysterious power of sex, which, being mysterious, is excessively dangerous and is guarded against by all sorts of taboos and by the penalty of death for transgression. We shall see illustrations of this later in the early codes ; but we may remark that " mob-law " and " lynch-law " are examples in civilized society ; and some panic-fear will generally be found at the source of them. Reigns of terror are well named ; for it is terror in the minds of the rulers which wakes up the ancient animal response to danger, viz. to kill that which is dangerous, the surest sanction being extinction. The change from the primitive attitude to the beginning of law is seen in the Code of Hammurabi,[1] where the death penalty, which is still imposed for offences against property, such as theft or helping a slave to escape, is in other cases set aside for various degrees of compensation. This is the common tendency in all the codes with the advance of civilization. There can be seen in it the operation of the civilized type of mind, which is not content to cut the Gordian knot of a problem by one simple drastic action, but brings together various considerations, such as the value of the man to the community, into a more abstract conception of money compensation.

In this simple application of conceptual thought to early forms of law there is also perceptible the germ of the ethical in the form of that early but tenacious idea of justice as a matter of equivalents, of identical values balanced against each other, which is its elementary form everywhere. We shall see more of

[1] R. W. Rogers, *Cuneiform Parallels to the Old Testament* (New York, 1926). (Cf. *passim.*)

this presently in relation to the *lex talionis* ; but we
may remark at this point on the entrance in other
very simple ways of moral considerations, and note
further that, where they appear, there is a religious
connexion. In both the prologue and the epilogue
to the Code of Hammurabi, where the king is claiming
to have been called by the gods to be the shepherd of
his people, he declares that he has been so called to
make justice and righteousness to prevail in the land
and to protect the weak against the strong.[1]   In a
much later text, belonging to the Neo-Babylonian
period within the last thousand years B.C., and
therefore approaching what we have called the
prophetic horizon with its great advances in religion
and ethics, a fragment called a " Prayer of the Raising
of the Hand to Ishtar," there are striking moral
qualities attributed to the deity as the basis of the
appeal. Thus, " thou judgest the cause of men with
justice and right " ; " thou regardest with mercy the
despised man ; thou settest right the down-trodden
every morning " ; " thou openest the bonds of all
slaves " ; " the unjust become just beholding thy
face." [2] Yet this prayer with its high ethical content
is embodied in an incantation designed to secure
recovery from sickness ; and in this mingling of
morals and religion with magic it is evident how near
the ancient civilized empire is to the primitive.
Nevertheless, man is here clearly on the great high
road which leads to the moralization of law in the
civilization of to-day, to its purification by ethical
considerations. For, indeed, the highest valuations
of the individual in modern times, like these faint
foregleams in the prayer to Ishtar, have been found

[1] *Cuneiform Parallels*, p. 399.   [2] *Op. cit.*, pp. 155–156.

in ethics inspired by religion ; and their expression in freedom of thought, speech and religion, and in such advances as the abolition of slavery and of the death penalty for comparatively light offences, is ultimately traceable to the prophetic horizon, and to the teaching of the prophets. These were not of one nation only but of several, though the truth came to them in different degrees ; but it is the view of a religious philosophy that they were justified in their unvarying consciousness that the illumination came to them by a Divine revelation.

2. *Psychological Origins*

In spite of what has just been said, there was nothing abrupt or magical in the transition from the primitive and tribal mind to the civilized ; and the great moral and religious thinkers, even, received their inspirations in the thought-forms of their age and race ; and so also the customary ways of thinking and acting on the part of the ancient food-gatherer and the early tribesman formed the moulds into which were run the laws of the early civilized communities. In illustrating this fact from two important characteristics of the primitive mind we may find some further light thrown upon the psychology of early law. One of these is what is known to anthropologists as the Law of Similarity in primitive magic, and the other is the magical connexion between the Person and Property.

The Law of Similarity is the idea found everywhere and in all ages among simple folk that like things are causally connected, that like is the cause of like. It is a mistaken inference, but it is extraordinarily

c

widespread over the world and through the ages. In caves in France and Spain there are engravings and paintings made by magician-artists of the Ice Ages, in which animals of the chase like the bison or the reindeer are portrayed with a wound in a vital part or with an arrow making towards the heart ; and the idea in them is that from these likenesses of that which they wished to happen there would go forth a mystical power to make it happen—that is, that the arrows of the tribesmen far across the plains would be directed infallibly to the heart of the hunted animal. In like manner the modern savage of Borneo or Central Africa dances his war-dance with a dramatic imitation of the coming raid or battle, believing that there is power in the dramatized likeness of the fight and the victory to make the victory happen on the morrow. So the tribal rain-maker imitates the breaking of clouds, the sound of thunder, and the falling raindrops ; and is sure that rain will come. It is the same principle in primitive medicine, on which toothache is cured by rubbing the bad tooth with the sound tooth of a dog, or pain in the eye removed by stroking with a stone resembling an eye ; and so forth. Without going further into the psychology of it, what interests us in the matter is the probability that this " law of similarity " in the primitive mind accounts for the law of retaliation, the *lex* or *jus talionis*, with which we are familiar in the Old Testament, and which occurs very frequently in the early laws of other nations.

The illusory law of similarity in magic is a mistaken application of the ordinary working of our minds in setting like things together so as to form them into classes and general ideas—which is the beginning of

all knowledge. The magical law of similarity which
induces the primitive to think that like has power to
make its like come to pass, as the magical picture of
success in the hunt makes it happen, or tooth cures
tooth or eye cures eye, makes for him another illusory
connexion in the earliest idea of law and justice,
namely, that punishment shall be the equivalent of
the crime, as like it as possible in order to be strictly
just. Hence the eye for an eye and a tooth for a tooth,
and the life for a life, of both the Hebrew Code and
the Laws of Hammurabi. In the latter there are
some curiously exact equivalents as if that gave
special satisfaction ; for instance, that if a man broke
into a house, he should be put to death before the
breach in the wall, and thrust into it ; and a man
stealing from a house on fire should be thrown into
that fire.[1] The inhumanity of this crude balancing
of like with like is seen in the law that if through bad
building the son of the owner of a house were killed,
the son of the builder should be put to death.[2] [3]

---

[1] *Op. cit.*, p. 408.

[2] *Ibid.*, p. 450.

[3] [That these extreme features are absent from the Hebrew
lex talionis shows the fundamental difference in ethical conception. The principle of exact equivalence was limited to the
person or animal who caused the injury or to the forewarned
owner of the notorious ox (see Exod. xxi. 29). In the latter case
money compensation was permissible, as the following verse 30
shows. Cf. also Deut. xxiv. 16, to the effect that every person
bears his own guilt. The substitution of money payment
(*mamon*) for the literal enforcement (*mammash*) is, in keeping with
a higher developed ethic, enjoined in the Mishnah. See further
Dr. Herford's paper, *below*, p. 104ff, and also *Jew. Enc.* x, *s.v.*
" Retaliation," and *Enc. Jud.* vii, *s.v.* " Gesetze," p. 359. Note,
moreover, that compensation was graded according to the impediment caused to the injured person in the execution of his
calling.—ED.]

The idea of strict equivalence as the first rude conception of justice in law, having its roots in the psychological connexion of similarity, expresses itself in pleasanter forms than the savage penalties just mentioned. It appears in the principle of reciprocity which takes form in the equal sharing of common possessions of the clan, which is often called " communism." This is a use of the word which is legitimate enough, if it is remembered that it co-exists always with many forms of private ownership by individuals in the clan, created by some relationship to the personality. The stranded whale is the property of the clan of Eskimos, and it is divided with scrupulous fairness ; but each man has a right to keep for himself as much driftwood as he can haul up unaided upon the ice ; and a stone placed upon it is an effective taboo, securing, under mystical penalties from unseen powers, that his ownership will not be interfered with. The same principle operates in barter and exchange. It is a well-known discovery of Professor Malinowski among the islanders of the South Seas that some of them have an elaborate system of exchange called the *Kula*, whereby articles of artistic value or adornment rather than the ordinary commodities of trade are exchanged among tribes over a wide area. Thus in the case of the Trobriand Islanders " Necklaces of red shell pass constantly along definite routes in a clockwise direction to the men who are in the Kula ; in the opposite direction there pass bracelets of white shell." [1] There are extensions of the same principle, as is pointed out by Thurnwald, to other systems of exchange, as when hill tribes in New Guinea exchange feather ornaments and stone weapons with the coast

[1] B. Malinowski, *Argonauts of the Western Pacific*, p. 82.

people in return for fish and shell ornaments.[1]
Dr. Thurnwald, in offering an explanation of these
systems of reciprocity, says : " The idea of requital,
like that of remuneration, appears to be one of the
original reactions of mankind. When applied to
wrong inflicted, the result is the blood feud, and when
applied to gifts, the reaction takes the form of exchange
or the development of trade." [2] The " original
reaction " may be yet further analysed psychologically
as the working of the " law of similarity " in the
primitive mind—that is to say, that connecting of like
things with like which is so fundamental to thought.
This is done causally in savage magic and ritual ; it
takes the form of strict equivalents in early justice and
in frequently cruel laws of retaliation ; it appears in
the useful shapes of mutual service in trade and
exchange ; and it finds noblest expression in the
reciprocity of loving your neighbour as yourself, and
in the imaginative sympathy of the Golden Rule.

3. Personality and Property

The psychological origin of early types of law in the
character of the thought of primitive man is illustrated
secondly by the various roots of the conception
of property. These are admirably analysed by
Beaglehole in his book on that subject.[3] Every
anthropologist has observed the tendency of the
primitive to regard anything that has been part of
himself, such as hair or nail-clippings, as still involved
with his personality, so that he can be magically

[1] R. Thurnwald, *Economics in Primitive Communities*, p. 152
(Oxford). [2] *Ibid.*, p. 141.
[3] Ernest Beaglehole, *Property*, pp. 135–136 (London, 1931).

influenced or injured through them, just as if they were sensitive parts of his body or gateways to his very soul. The same extension of the personality to what has been closely associated with it accounts for the simpler ideas of property, of possession in tools, weapons, and in the products of one's own labour. There is nothing recondite or " mystical " about the psychology implied. It is our own thought employed in simple, childlike, rustic, and blundering ways, and influenced more directly by impulse and feeling. Thus there is an intelligible root of the sense of owner-ship in the idea of William James that " a great part of our feelings about what is ours is due to the fact that we live *closer* to our own things and so feel them more thoroughly and deeply." [1]   The primitive mind, too, welcomes simple ways of solving its problems because it sees no others.   When a primitive food-gatherer finds an unowned fruit tree, and makes it his property by laying a stone at its root, he is doing the same thing as the schoolboy who " bags " the corner seat in a railway carriage, or the country lad who claims first choice of the eggs in a nest which he has found ; and in each case the rule is obeyed like a law. All three are employing the category of " firstness," of being there first, as decisive of right of possession. There is nothing ethical about it ; but it is decisive, and saves the fatigue of thought—an important matter for simple and primitive minds.[2]   It has amazing ramifications, not only into the conventions of school-boys and the perilous taboos of savages, but into the solemn legalities of primogeniture, inheritance of estates and empires, and the possession of newly

---

[1] *Principles of Psychology* (1910), i. 377.
[2] J. Murphy, *Primitive Man*, pp. 242 ff. (Oxford, 1927).

explored countries on the ground of being the first to plant a flag there.

Thus for the primitive and tribal mind a man's " rights " to things are determined by such simple concrete factors as being " there first," or feelings of close association with one's " own things," or the strong satisfaction of the creative impulse in anything one has made or produced, or the sacredness of the land where one's dead are buried and in which their spirits are still somehow present ; and such laws as there are concern these. But it is when the civilized mind with its capacity for abstract, conceptual thought and for ethical judgment supervenes upon the earlier ways of thought, that such rights are swept into the ambit of moral right and wrong, and ethical reasons are found for them. Further, within the horizon of the ancient empires in which that civilized mind appeared, religion becomes to a degree a personal relationship to divine powers ; and these divine beings, the gods of the higher polytheisms and of the incipient monotheisms, are regarded as supremely influential upon life and authoritative for conduct. Hence the authors of those early collections of existing rules of crime and punishment which are scarcely yet codes refer them generally to the authority of high gods. Finally, within the prophetic horizon, the great religious teachers and originators, such as Akhenaten, Zoroaster, Moses and the Hebrew prophets, Socrates, Jesus and Muhammad, whether in laying down principles for the individual conscience, or for the conduct of a nation, or in teaching and manifesting an inner spirit which is of universal application, tend to regard their communication as divinely inspired, in other words, as Revelation.

4. *Law and Revelation*

We may conclude this introductory study by considering in a summary way the relation of law in its
early forms and development to this aspect of religion.
Revelation implies a certain religious point of view or
philosophy centring in the theistic conception of a
supreme Personality whose will it is to reveal Himself
to man. The discovery of the fact of evolution as
applied to the world of nature and to human life and
history necessitates the conception of a gradual
revelation of God in His nature and His will for
mankind, proportioned to the powers of man, to whom
the revelation is made, to perceive it. An indication
of the acceptance of this position in many various
quarters is given in a leading article in the scientific
journal *Nature* [1] recently. Referring to the lately published report of the Church of England's Commission
on Doctrine, and in particular to its application of the
principle of development both to the method of God's
creation of the world and to man's apprehension of
religious truth which is embodied in his theology, the
writer said : " It may seem that to hold such a view
of the relation of the evolution of theological dogma
to the development of scientific thought is to make
the validity of religious belief dependent upon the
finite intelligence of man and to be incompatible with
the tenets of a religion which takes its stand upon
divine revelation. Yet is it not possible to regard
both the growth of scientific knowledge and the
development of dogma each in its respective field as
two sides, two aspects of the same process—the search

[1] Vol. 141, p. 531.

for truth in which the Divine purpose is revealed gradually to man *pari passu* with the preparation of his heart and intellect to receive it with understanding ? " The evolution of law for man, most clearly in its loftiest moral and spiritual forms, more obscurely and yet perhaps not less truly in the secular ordering of human life, is a particular case of revelation in the sense just outlined. To the theistic philosophy which finds God at work creatively in the universe and in the life of man, law, from its first expression in the needs and impulses (both self-regarding and altruistic) of subhuman, animal instinct, through the ever more varied choices presented to the growing intelligence, and thence onward to the highest moral and spiritual imperatives, is at once a revelation by the creating Power, and at the same time is a series of discoveries, imaginative integrations, and first crudely and later wisely reasoned co-ordinations of the created mind.

We may illustrate this finally from the early stages of man's religious and social development. The earliest type of religion known to us is a perception of something mysterious, a sense of mystery in things not understood, to which man ascribes *power* to affect his life for evil or for good. The Power (the capital letter is justified by the unique attitude of awe which man takes to the Power) is not personal ; but by a natural anthropomorphism *life* is ascribed to it, especially if it moves ; and it has *will* because it can do or not do things when it is requested by prayer or induced by charm or spell. Such law as the primitive food-gatherer or hunter knows at this stage—that is, his customary rules of conduct—is closely associated with these mysterious powers which he partly fears and partly trusts. They are the serious " sanctions " of his taboos, and protect his property and avenge his wrongs with dire penalties. These powers also lay down the law for his magico-religious rites, and (what is often forgotten) their beneficence moves him to gratitude and a dim sense of obligation. Thus in great part his religious life is the fountain of his moral life ; and, involved in that universal belief in mysterious, unseen power which is the natural germ of all religion and the first ray of the dawn of Revelation, there are the first imperatives of Law. To go yet further to the more advanced condition of tribalism this may be said. For a philosophy which holds that all man's acquisitions in the higher values are at the same time gifts from the Divine, the great virtue of the tribe, its solidarity, its sense of kinship in which the god may be included, when it broadens out into the conception of brotherhood and the obligations of altruism, may be regarded as such a gift. When, lastly, in Akhenaten this sense of the kinship of mankind makes it possible for him to regard his Sun-god as the creator not merely of Egypt but of " Syria and Cush," that is at least a remarkable inspiration ; and when the prophets of Judaism and Christianity declare that the greatest laws which govern human conduct are love of God and love of the brother man, religion declares that this is at once a triumph of human genius and a Revelation of God.

II

LAW AND RELIGION IN BABYLONIA AND ASSYRIA

BY

T. FISH

II

THE subject of this paper will be treated under a special aspect. That aspect is defined by the object of the whole course of these lectures, which is set out in the syllabus thus : " the relation between revealed Law and Religion," or, as is said later in the same place, " the divine command claimed to be made known in Revelation and human custom necessitating human law."

The area of discussion is therefore very limited. It does not include an outline of the religion of Babylonia and Assyria : its pantheon, its evolution, its diffusion, its expression in cult and ritual. Nor does it include an outline of the rules of law : their origin, their provisions, their value, the time and place of their enactment and authority, or the details of legal procedure.

By way of preamble we recall that the ancient history of the valley of the Euphrates and Tigris is known. We have more than an outline : we have a general history. Some chapters in that long story are more detailed than others. But no chapter lacks detail of persons, movements, motives ; of religion, politics, economics ; of language, science and art. It is the general history of an advanced civilization—of groups lying along the rivers and arable lands of Mesopotamia, with organized religion, commerce and ancient tradition ; with developed life and institutions in cities of long standing ; with strong feeling for the local god and his property the city or state, that is, patriotism.

The great historical epochs are easily defined :

(i) The third millennium B.C. : Sumerian with a Semitic interlude.

(ii) The second millennium B.C. : Semitic with Babylon as the centre of political power.

(iii) The first millennium B.C. till 538 B.C. : Semitic with Assyria as the centre of power, though challenged often, till the Fall of Nineveh, 612 B.C., when authority passed to Babylon and from there was exercised till the Fall of Babylon in 538 B.C.

We must mark two things if we are to appreciate the background of Religion and Law in this area. The first derives from the geographical situation. The River Valley lands which we call Mesopotamia were not a necessary highway between continents as were Syria and Palestine. Hence there was not in Mesopotamia, especially in the south, such a fusion of peoples and cultures as obtained in Syria and in Palestine, which were natural corridor lands. Yet there was fusion : fusion by peaceful immigration, by trade, and by more violent penetration through invasion and conquest. In the third millennium Semites mingled with the non-Semitic Sumerians and temporarily dominated them. This dominion was overthrown, but only temporarily. It was re-established finally and permanently towards the end of the third millennium. In the second millennium Babylonia was Semitic, though the rulers and the court at Babylon were non-Semitic (Kassite) for several centuries.

And yet, in spite of such political discontinuity, there can be traced a continuity though not an identity of culture from, say, 3000 B.C. till Babylonia ceased to be an independent political state in 538 B.C. This is especially true in the matter of religion and, to a lesser degree, in the matter of law.

The second factor worthy of remark as an element of the background derives from the political situation. In Mesopotamia, as in the whole world of the ancient Near East, *the* political unit was the city- or the temple-state. In the early days each city or town in which men lived had its own political constitution as well as its own gods and its own laws. The earliest wars were wars between cities, as, for example, between Lagash and its neighbour Umma. Even in the days of " Empire " under the rulers of Ur, *c.* 2300 B.C., there was merely external unity. Each city continued to have its own chief deity, its own calendar, its own economic organization and its own customs regulating business contracts which were contracts in law. And even in the much later age of the great Assyrian Empire, local patriotism, even local autonomy, was claimed and granted and exercised in centres of historical, religious and political importance, both in Assyria proper and in Babylonia, in some degree.

As is well known, many of these city states, centres of Sumerian, Akkadian, Babylonian and Assyrian life, have been excavated by official expeditions under foreign authority—British, French, German and American—or have been " explored " by native diggers in search for building material for their own houses or for antiquities for the foreign market. In consequence we possess tens of thousands of documents, usually clay tablets written in Sumerian, Akkadian, Kassite, Babylonian and Assyrian.

The matter of these documents is of the most varied sort : historical, religious, scientific, economic, and even correspondence private and official. Further details of this literature need not be given here. Enough to state that in the matter with which we are here concerned, religion and law, it is abundant. Indeed we may say that this abundance of literary remains shows clearly that the two institutions which are paramount in the ancient culture of Mesopotamia are those of religion and law.

It is obvious that from this mass of material a selection must be made, and according to some principle. In this instance the principle of selection is suggested by the circumstance that this series of lectures is concerned chiefly with the Torah, with the Jewish Law. Accordingly throughout I have had in mind those qualities, and only those, traditionally attaching to the Law and the laws of Israel. Tradition asserts that the Law is religious and revealed. If this line of approach implies comparison between Babylonian and Assyrian laws and the Law of Israel, the comparison will not be explicit ; it will be suggested, not emphasised. Nor will the comparison be a comparison of details, that is, of specific law with specific law. That has been done *ad nauseam*, and not yet finally. And in a lecture which is concerned with the history and authority of law in Babylonia and Assyria it would be irrelevant.

The description of the object of this course, " the relation between revealed Law and Religion," contains three terms : Revelation, Religion and Law.

I shall treat of them in this order : Religion, Revelation and Law. In the first part I shall expose these elements as they are found in the documented culture of Babylonia and Assyria. Of these elements one, Law, will receive more attention than the other two. In the second part I shall try to set forth briefly the historical relations between Religion and Law with special relation to the aspect of Babylonian and Assyrian Law as " revealed."

Without attempting a definition we may describe Religion amongst the peoples of Mesopotamia as a *bond* between the inhabitants of a city or a kingdom and the parental god of the city or kingdom. The family of men was closely and consciously *bound* to the family of the god from whom and from whose divine relatives all things and all men derive. Such a " bond " implies an attitude of mind ; a way of looking at the universe ; a conception of gods and of men ; a plan of the world, its origin, its vicissitudes, its meaning. All this is matter of creed. The formal and more or less explicit expression of this creed was expressed in Babylonia and Assyria in native cosmogonies, in prayers, in litanies, in hymns as well as in the formal lists of gods and goddesses, and even in the " secular " documents such as contracts, sales, laws, and accounts of public works and foreign wars. No literature of any age from any centre of any sort lacks religious content—that is, data which bear witness to contemporary religion in the sense of the bond between the family of men and the family of the gods.

In all this literature there is no explicit philosophizing about the nature of the gods, but there is much explicit description of the ways of the gods with one another and with men. There is nothing which

D

might be called " philosophy " of the essential nature
of man, though there is a proverb " Man is the
shadow of god, the slave is the shadow of a man, but
the king is like god " ; but there is much about the
ways in which a man must walk, that is, practical
ethics. But in this lecture we are not concerned so
much with ethics as with law—that is, rules promulgated by authority in a political society.

It belongs to our inquiry to ask whether Babylonian
and Assyrian religious thought included the notion of
Revelation.

In the large sense of the term Revelation denotes
divine collaboration with human intelligence. This
large sense is not considered here. In the strict sense
Revelation is the manifestation of a fact or truth by
a formal word of God. It is the strict sense that is
considered here.

We may further distinguish revelation according to
its object. The object revealed may be the existence
of a god of whose existence an individual person or a
group of persons was ignorant at the time when it
was revealed. Or, it may be some truth, whether
practical or theoretical, of which an individual person
or a group of persons was ignorant at the time when
it was revealed.

No cuneiform text published so far states explicitly
or implicitly that a deity previously unknown to men
made himself or herself known to them. But there is
abundant evidence in the myths, in the historical
literature and in the religious literature of Babylonia
and Assyria that the people of those lands thought
that the gods made known to men facts and truths of
which they were ignorant at the time when such
knowledge was communicated to them.

For example : in the Babylonian mythology, the god Enki or Ea gives wisdom to Adapa, and Ea is the teacher of mankind in all the arts and crafts of civilization and in letters ; in the flood story Ea instructs the hero Ziusudu how to build a boat ; he hears the voice of Ea ; and in the Sumerian Poem of Paradise the gods give to man the more abstract notions of justice and righteousness. According to Berossus, Oannes emerged from the Persian Gulf to teach mathematics to the early inhabitants of Babylonia.

Predictions are the word of God. Man's destiny is made known by the writing in the skies given by the hand of Nabu the god of revelation, whose consort Tashmet is revelation itself.

In passing we may note that the divine words in the matter of destiny are arbitrary and mutable. This background of impermanence in divine sentences and commands suggests that we must not expect permanence in the matter of laws which, like destiny judgments, are from the gods.

It is clear therefore from the above very short selection of data that the peoples of Mesopotamia had the idea of Revelation in the sense of communication of knowledge by the deities to men ; knowledge which related to gods, the world and mankind.

We pass to the third and the central element of this sketch : Law. Two things must be remarked at the outset. First : though we can speak of Babylonian and Assyrian religion as of a unity, we cannot speak of Babylonian and Assyrian Law as of a unity. The gods are constants ; their works not so. Secondly : Babylonian and Assyrian Law does not show a *progressive* evolution. For example, it is claimed that the juridical conceptions of the Neo-Babylonian times are inferior to those of the First Dynasty of Babylon hundreds of years earlier.

In the present state of our knowledge it is customary to divide generously the periods of law in Mesopotamia somewhat as follows :

In Babylonia : (i) the Sumerian period within which was a Semitic interlude with a legal spirit proper to itself ; (ii) the First Dynasty of Babylon ; (iii) the Kassite period ; (iv) the Neo-Babylonian period.

In Assyria : (i) Palæo-Assyrian (second half of the third millennium), known by evidence from Asia Minor ; (ii) Middle Assyrian period, from which we have a collection of laws ; (iii) Neo-Assyrian times.

Until recently the Code of Hammurabi monopolized the attention of scholars and students of ancient law. Its discovery in 1901–02 was a major sensation.   Its contents bearing on property, the family and the *lex talionis* were seen to be of first importance *in se* and in relation to the only other known ancient Semitic code of laws, that of Israel.   But it must be said that the importance of the Code of Hammurabi has been exaggerated.   The exaggeration arose from the fact that the Code of Hammurabi was studied in isolation. It was considered apart from its contexts in the history and practice of law in Babylonia and Assyria.

There was never any *a priori* reason to think that it was the only one of its kind native to Mesopotamia. Nor was there ever any reason to think that it was certainly original.   It was merely new—that is, new to us.   And at this date there is abundant evidence to suggest that it was neither unique nor original.

The evidence is of two sorts : (i) Law in practice

before Hammurabi, that is, before 1900 B.C. ; (ii) explicit rules of law before Hammurabi. Before the Code was put together there had been in the land of its origin almost a thousand years of busy life ; of organized society in the various city states ; of labour and trade ; of buying and selling ; of claim and counter-claim ; of dispute and decision ; of abuses and reforms : that is, of Law in practice.

Early in the history of Lagash, Urukagina the royal reformer [1] set aside customs which then obtained in the state. " He restored the ancient decisions (of the city's god) and gave currency to the word which his king Ningirsu had spoken to him." [2] Indeed the custody of the law and the right ordering of society was the chief duty of kings and of all political authorities. The first king of the Third Dynasty of Ur " according to the just law of the Sun god (Utu Shamash) made justice to prevail." [3] Lipit Ishtar of Isin " established justice in the land of Sumer and Akkad." [4] Similar claims might be quoted from the records of other Sumerian kings before Hammurabi.

But in addition to such general statements from individual rulers we read of judges (rarely mentioned before Ur III), of numerous accounts of case trials, of contracts before witnesses and conditioned. From all these it is clear that fixed standards or rules obtained in the various cities. These rules governed business transactions. They were the grounds of appeal

[1] See full texts and discussion by Deimel, *Orientalia*, No. 2, pp. 1–31.

[2] *Die S(umerischen) und A(kkadischen) K(önigsinschriften)*, 50, 8, 7 f.

[3] *S.A.K.* 188, i. 1 : 15 f.

[4] *Yale Oriental Series*, I. No. 27, 24 f. ; *Ur Royal Inscriptions*, No. 106, 24 f.

between contending parties and were the rules which governed the decisions of courts. The rules can sometimes be deduced from the local legal practice wherever the evidence is, as in the period of Ur III, sufficiently abundant.

All the data referred to above belong to the Sumerian age. They relate to the customs of a swarming, highly organized, technical, commercial folk with an intricate subdivision of labour and definite class distinctions. All this involved conflict and stress around concrete realities such as things and persons. All subject to Law—that is, to the local rules of the respective city states.

The second kind of evidence consists of explicit rules of law set forth as such. The laws were formulated in the form of conditional sentences in the third person (" If a man " or, as under Urukagina, " the man who "). The sentence first stated the contingency and followed by a statement of the consequences in law.

The earliest explicit rules governing the body politic, of which we have contemporary evidence, date from the time of Urukagina of Lagash (early third millennium). Others are of later composition but are probably to be dated at the close of the Sumerian age, that is, towards the end of the third millennium. Of this latter age we have about thirty laws or sentences. The history behind them is not yet known, but it is possible that our knowledge of that history will increase. It may be mere coincidence that a Nippur tablet of the Third Dynasty of Ur [1] prescribes the same fine for a labourer who stands idle as is

[1] Cf. Fish in *Journal of the American Oriental Society*, vol. 56, No. 4.

prescribed in one of the laws of the *ana ittišu* series, which is one of our chief sources for explicit law before Hammurabi.

The data we have given of the practice of law and of systematic rules of law represent a long history of legal decision antecedent to the Code of Hammurabi. They are interesting in themselves and, more to our present purpose, they permit of comparison [1] with the Code of Hammurabi. Such comparison helps us to a right judgment of the Code. All or nearly all the express Sumerian laws are matters of rule in Hammurabi's Code promulgated after the end of the pure Sumerian age. This fact, aided by reasonable assumptions, leads us to say that the laws of Hammurabi are a compilation based entirely on preceding laws. Those earlier laws are certainly Sumerian. Some, perhaps, are Akkadian, though we have no Akkadian laws in Akkadian language previous to Hammurabi. The earlier Sumerian laws were adapted to the Semitic conditions which now prevailed in the land.

It is doubtful whether the Code was original even in respect of language. The phrase *ina pî mâtim* is usually translated " in the speech of the land." But this translation has been challenged.[2]

As to the force or actuality of the laws of Hammurabi in his own time and later, the facts are : (i) We do not know whether the Code operated throughout Babylonia and the territory under Babylonian rule. I doubt it. Recall what was said earlier about the local patriotisms born of centuries of city-state life ;

---

[1] See Langdon, *Journal of the Royal Asiatic Society*, 1920, pp. 489–514.

[2] By Eilers, *O.L.Z.* 1931, S. 933.

the centuries of local courts and local decisions. Moreover there is evidence that legal business was transacted according to local laws and local right. (ii) There is evidence to show that rules were in force in the land additional [1] to and sometimes contrary [2] to those laid down in the Code of Hammurabi. An important example of opposition is in the matter of *tappûtum* or partnership.[3] The partnership was between a creditor and one, more usually two debtors. The arrangement was that the creditor shared the gains with the debtors but only the debtors bore the losses. This is contrary to the Code of Hammurabi, which decrees that the partners shall share both gains and losses. In this matter at least the Code was a norm which never had any reality in practice.

It would seem that Hammurabi was conservative. He did not begin with a *tabula rasa*, but attempted to conserve precedent and its advice. He was for the authority of tradition.

He legislated " for the future and for all time." Like Rousseau, Cousin, Jouffrey, Danuron, Jules Simon, Janet and Care—but these on the basis of human reason alone—he thought to impose rules of conduct valid for all time ; they for all countries, he only for his own.

He expresses a wish, even a command backed up by sanctions, that his successors and his people regard his Code as a fixed code : just as on the continent of Europe during the twelfth and thirteenth centuries A.D. the Law of Justinian was regarded by the com-

---

[1] Cf. Schorr, *Altbabylonische Rechtsurkunden*, i, S. 100 ; 114 ; ii, S. 14, etc.

[2] *loc. cit.*, S. 134.

[3] Eilers, *Gesellschaftsformen im altbabylonischen Recht*, S. 16.

mentators " as a fixed code binding them almost as if the Emperor were still ruling." [1]

(iii) In later centuries the Code of Hammurabi enjoyed a great reputation. Copies of it have been found at many places and in many epochs down to the Neo-Babylonian times. But this reputation does not seem to have rested on the juridical value of the Code. Reverence for the past and especially for the remote past was a characteristic of the peoples of ancient Mesopotamia. And they were intelligent enough to appreciate the grandeur of the achievement which the Code is. Its enactments were no longer the legal norm, but it was surely more than a literary relic.

So far there has been mention only of Sumerian laws and of the Semitic Code of Hammurabi. There is, however, abundant evidence of other laws in set form and in practice, in different times and areas of Mesopotamian history. For the purposes of our subject we need only remark that their existence indicates that what we have already said of Hammurabi's Code is true : it was not inviolable and it was not permanent. And the same is true of them.

We come now to the last and chief point which this short study has in view : the relation between Law and Religion in ancient Mesopotamia.

Fustel de Coulanges held that religion is the source of law and of all relations between men and the things of men in the world of the Greeks and the Romans. A similar thesis could be defended in respect of the ancient Semitic world. In the matter of Law we might assume, even without the express evidence of the texts, that the Babylonians and Assyrians traced

[1] Lord Justice Slesser, *The Law*, p. 8.

their laws to religion. They, as all things else, were the gift of the gods. But there is explicit evidence that the peoples of ancient Mesopotamia thought of laws in relation to the gods. We have already quoted texts from the Sumerian age which are pertinent here (see p. 37). And throughout the historical times of Babylonia and Assyria, Shamash and the mother goddess in her various forms were deities most usually associated with right and justice and laws.

In the Semitic age the only explicit statement that formal rules of law came from the gods is found in the Code of Hammurabi. The later Assyrian and Neo-Babylonian codes do not assert this.

As to Hammurabi there seems to be some discrepancy in his statements on this point. In places he seems to attribute the laws to himself. He affirms that he was named by the gods " to make justice shine in the land." [1] Hence, " I established right and law in the land." [2] And so, his long list of laws are " statutes of justice which Hammurabi the powerful king set up, by which he gave to the earth true salvation and good government." [3] These are " the law of the land which I gave." [4] But elsewhere he says " I am Hammurabi, the king of justice to whom Shamash has given rules of law," [5] thus attributing the laws to the Sun-god.

It might be argued that the representation on the obverse of the Code decides the matter. It is true that this representation is usually said to be a picture of the god, Shamash, giving the laws of the Code to Hammurabi. But it is by no means certain that the picture of itself and primarily represents the god in

[1] C.H. 1, 27-34.   [2] C.H. 5, 20 f.   [3] C.H. R. 24, 1-8.
[4] C.H. R. 25, 68.   [5] C.H. R. 25, 95 f.

the act of giving laws. We see Hammurabi standing reverentially before the seated deity, Shamash, who holds in his hands a staff and a ring. Such a picture is not new. The reader may be referred to the great stele of Ur Nammu found at Ur [1] and of a time more than two hundred years before Hammurabi. Here the scene shows a king standing before his god and performing an act of ritual. The god is seated and in his hand he holds the ring, the staff and the measuring line. It will be observed that though the occasions of the two steles are different, yet the relative positions and attitudes of king and god, and the ring and the staff are common to both. The ring and the staff are the insignia of royalty. It is these that the god is handing to Hammurabi. The picture expresses primarily what the prologue of the Code expresses in words : that Hammurabi's kingly power is from heaven. " Kingship descended from heaven " [2] was an article of the creed of Babylonians and Assyrians. The power of kingship included the power to give laws to the land and its people. And there is no convincing argument against the view that the picture in representing the giving of kingship includes the giving of laws. But the giving of laws by the god to the king is not immediately represented by the picture.

It has been said [3] of the Code of Hammurabi and of Mesopotamian laws in general that they " have nothing to do with religion. The only relation which they have with religion consists in the fact that they are considered to have been given to the king by the

[1] See *The Sumerians* (Woolley), frontispiece and p. 134 f.

[2] W–B. 444, col. 1, line 41, in *Oxford Edition of Cuneiform Texts*, vol. ii.

[3] Furlani, *La Civiltà Babilonese e Assira*, p. 410.

god Shamash. Infringement of the laws does not constitute a religious infringement or a sin except in a very secondary sense.[1] The punishments are purely secular."

The statement as the author explains it cannot be accepted without qualification. The words " have nothing to do with religion " would seem to introduce into Babylonian and Assyrian thought a conception, a distinction which is alien to it. The Babylonians and Assyrians made no clear distinction between civil and religious. In their thought all power is religious in its source, in its purpose and in its action. They knew nothing of our distinction between civil power and religious authority ; between the powers temporal and the powers spiritual ; between religious life and " secular " conduct. To plough a field, to dig a canal, to go to war and the like were, in their minds, religious acts ; as religious as to offer prayers, to consult omens, to dedicate a temple. And the promulgation of laws by political authority and the observance of them by the members of the body politic were, in a real sense, religious acts also.

SELECTED BIBLIOGRAPHY OF GENERAL WORKS

A. Religion of Babylonia and Assyria :
  MEISSNER : *Babylonien und Assyrien*, 2 vols. (1925).
  FURLANI : *La Religione Babilonese-Assira*, 2 vols. (1928–29).
  DHORME : *La Religion assyro-babylonienne.*
  —— *Choix de Textes Religieux Assyro-Babyloniens* (1907).

B. Laws of Babylonia and Assyria :
  FURLANI : *Leggi dell' Asia Anteriore Antica* (1929).
  —— *La Civiltà Babilonese e Assira*, cap. xi (1929).
  DEIMEL : *Codex Hammurabi* (1930).
  MEISSNER : *Babylonien und Assyrien*, vol. i, pp. 149–183.

---

[1] But in his *La Religione Bab.-Assir.*, ii, p. 318, Furlani seems to go further.

III

LAW AND RELIGION IN ISRAEL

BY

H. WHEELER ROBINSON

SYNOPSIS

Introduction : Custom, morality and law ; the modern separation of law and religion not primitive ; the divorce of law from religion in Rome and Greece, and of individual morality and religion from the law of the state. In Israel, law was taken up into religion as a permanent quality of it.

1. *The Development of Law.*
    i. The difference between *Torah* and *Nomos.*
    ii. The meaning of Torah (priest, prophet, sage) and its final use for " revelation."

2. *The Origins and Source of Law.*
    i. The case-law of the lay judge (*mishpaṭim*) added to the priestly and prophetic *toroth.*
    ii. Revelation does not stand or fall by its means of mediation.
    iii. Wisdom and the inclusive view of revelation pointing to ultimate " value-judgments."

3. *Law and Ideal.*
    i. Contrast of the Greek ideal of due measure ; the law of nature ; the upward movement of the " ideal " to the " idea " ; philosophy rather than religion.
    ii. Pedagogic necessity of law ; education.

4. *The Adequacy of Israel's Law.*
    i. Written law necessarily temporary in form ; its re-interpretation by " oral tradition."
    ii. Law unable to reach the inner life—till it becomes *Torah* (*berith* and *ḥeśed* ; the command to love).
    iii. Mixture of moral and ritual elements (Montefiore) ; yet ritual may become sacramental.
    iv. " In God the law is alive " (Dale).

5. *Law in Relation to the Revelation in History.*
    The temporal and the eternal.

III

LAW AND RELIGION IN ISRAEL

BACON has reminded us that " Custome is the Principall Magistrate of Man's life," and he goes on to point out how greatly its influence is increased when the custom of the individual is also that of the society to which he belongs : " For there Example teacheth ; Company comforteth ; Emulation quickeneth ; Glory raiseth." But custom is not the only factor in our ordinary life, even though it is the largest. In all men it can be modified by a greater or less degree of morality, since custom implies some obligation as well as habit.[1] Such morality may become strong enough to enable the individual to rebel against the tyranny of custom, whether in his own life or in that of the society. In some men this individual morality is reinforced by religious faith. On the other hand, custom is partly entrenched in law, itself often the formal ratification of custom by the society or its representatives and rulers. It is true enough, as Lord Macmillan [2] has recently reminded us, that our daily life, from morning to night, is hedged round, for its security and its amenities, by a very complex network of law. But we are rarely made conscious of this, unless it be by a rating or income-tax

[1] E. Westermarck, *The Origin and Development of the Moral Ideas*, i. 159.

[2] *Law and Other Things*, pp. 268, 269.

demand, by new traffic regulations, or by a glance at
the report of some trial in the newspaper. The law
of the land forms the remote circumference of our life,
whilst our religion, if we have any, is the centre, for
it is our personal affair, which the law cannot touch.
We no more think of confusing law and religion than
of interchanging a policeman and a clergyman
because they both wear uniform.

This sharp separation of law and religion, so usual
in our modern world, is found in the ancient world
only as the result of a gradual development. In
primitive societies, law in the form of ruling custom
was frequently reinforced by religious sanctions ; the
customs of the group, in fact, were largely a form of
its religion, whether they related to non-moral ritual
or to what we should call morality. But in both
Roman and Greek history we can trace the gradual
divorce of law from religion, in characteristically
different ways. In Rome, religion was controlled by
the college of pontifices and the college of augurs.[1]
The pontifices, succeeding to the former power of
the king, were, in Warde Fowler's words, " the sole
depositaries of the religious law in the period during
which the civil law was being slowly disentangled
from it." [2] The publication of the XII Tables in the
middle of the fifth century, though including both the
ius divinum and the *ius civile*, ultimately enabled Roman
civil law to attain a separate existence. In the fourth
century the administration of this civil law passed
into lay hands.[3] " The old State religion remained,
but in stunted form and with paralysed vitality ;

---

[1] W. Warde Fowler, *The Religious Experience of the Roman
People*, pp. 270 ff.
[2] *Op. cit.*, p. 272.   [3] *Op. cit.*, p. 279.

Rome was the scene of an *arrested religious development.*" [1]
. . . " Religion was effectually divorced from life
and morality." [2] Even from the beginning, however,
the pontifices and the augurs were subordinate to the
imperium of the king and his successors, the magistrates. " Rome was never hierarchically governed." [3]

In the Greek cities the development followed a
different course, though to the same end. In the
primitive Greek group " Themis is simply the tribal
rule or custom, the thing that is lawful because it is
always done, that is obligatory because it is always
done," [4] and Themis is linked to the Delphic oracle.
Later on, the primitive group was replaced by the
city, where the ideal was the welfare of the individual,
and the policy has been described by Vinogradoff as
" a cultural socialism." [5] The law of the *polis* was
conceived as the gift of the gods to men, though it was
actually worked out, on the basis of custom, by the
Athenian democracy. The criticism of this law and
religion came from those poets and philosophers
through whom the higher morality and religion of
Greece was developed. Antigone, for example, is
shown as one who has to choose between the law of
the State and the moral law, whilst Socrates, who
" spent his life in convincing the Athenians, not of sin,
but of ignorance," [6] is represented as saying to the
men of Athens, " I shall obey God rather than you "
(*Apol.* 29).

On the other hand, in Israel the course and the

---

[1] *Op. cit.*, p. 287.   [2] *Op. cit.*, p. 288.   [3] *Op. cit.*, p. 302.
[4] G. Murray in *The Individual in East and West* (ed. by E. R.
Hughes), p. 39.
[5] *Encyclopædia of Religion and Ethics*, vii. 848.
[6] R. W. Livingstone, *The Pageant of Greece*, p. 271.

E

issue of the development were very different. There
was a similar background of tribal custom linked to
religion, but the religion of Israel showed unique
features from an early date. The result of its intensity
was that law came to be included *within* religion,[1]
instead of being divorced from it, as in Rome and
Greece. The history of this development in Israel
can be sufficiently outlined by an account of the use
of the most important word for " law," viz. "torah,"
which ultimately became the most important term for
the religious basis of Judaism. But it should be
remembered throughout this discussion that we are
concerned with the course of the development in
Israel, rather than the result in the post-canonical
Judaism.

1. *The Development of Law*

The common rendering of the term " torah " by
" law " goes back, through the translation " lex " of
the Vulgate, to the " nomos " of the Septuagint. But
as Professor C. H. Dodd has shown, in an excellent
study in *The Bible and the Greeks*, this translation of
" torah " resulted in a falsely legalistic emphasis for
the Hellenistic Jews. *Nomos* properly denoted custom,
hardening into " law," with no necessary reference to
a legislative authority. " It is rather an immanent or
underlying principle of life and action " (p. 25). But
torah meant originally direction or instruction, especially as given by God through priests and prophets.
So far as these rules of living became codified, they
became law in our sense, and offered common ground

[1] See, further, my essay on " The Theology of the Old Testament " in *Record and Revelation*.

with *nomos*. But just as *nomos* in addition to this meaning also meant " principle," as *torah* did not, so *torah* also meant " teaching," as *nomos* did not. The fundamental meaning of *torah* as " direction " or " instruction " probably owes its origin to the use of the sacred oracle or lot, administered by the priests.[1] Joshua (xviii. 6) is represented as saying, with reference to the division of Canaan, " I will cast lots for you here before Yahweh our God." The verb used (*yarah*) is that from which the noun " torah " is derived, and is regularly used for teaching or direction. Thus, when we classify the 217 instances of the use of the noun *torah* in the Old Testament (omitting the corrupt instance in 2 Sam. vii. 19), it is natural to begin with these oral decisions of the priests. Fourteen instances of these are found, and they may be best illustrated by Deut. xxxiii. 10 (in the Blessing of Moses), not later than the eighth century. Here it is said of Levi, " They shall teach Jacob thy judgments and Israel thy *torah*," the verb " teach " and the noun *torah* being derived from the same root, whilst there is a direct reference to the *Thummim* and *Urim*, the sacred oracle, in a previous verse (8). With such priestly decisions we may link those of Moses, in the scene which pictures him as a nomadic sheik, administering the rough and ready justice of the desert by oral decisions (Exod. xviii. 16, 20) which go back, on occasion, to the divine oracle.[2] Later on, we hear of similar decisions made by associated priests and

---

[1] So Jirku, *Das weltliche Recht im Alten Testament*, p. 11, and many other scholars. The rejection of this origin by Begrich (" Die priesterliche Tora," *Beiheft* 66 *d. Zeitschrift f. alttest. Wissenschaft*, p. 68) is quite unconvincing.

[2] So G. B. Gray, *Sacrifice in the Old Testament*, pp. 206 ff. He shows the *priestly* activity of Moses in this narrative.

lay judges (Deut. xvii. 8–13 ; 2 Chron. xix. 8–11).[1]
No doubt such decisions were often made on the
practical ground of precedent or common sense,
though they might be recognized as of divine
appointment.

But we find the term *torah* also used of the teaching
of the prophets,[2] derived not from the physical
decision of the sacred lot, but from the psychical
source of the prophetic consciousness.   Thus Isaiah is
bidden to bind up his testimony and to seal his *torah*
in written form, after its oral utterance has been disregarded, and to entrust this writing to his disciples
(viii. 16).   Here the *torah* is his demand for faith in
God.   A further interesting extension of this use for
general teaching is found in the Wisdom writers, e.g.
Prov. xiii. 14, " The *torah* of the wise is a fountain of
life, to depart from the snares of death."   In all, some
59 instances may be gathered into these groups, all
used of some form of teaching or direction.

The remaining 158 examples refer to written instruction, formally given and accepted as " law." [3]
In 32 of them, the reference is to particular " laws,"
such as the *torah* of the burnt offering (Lev. vi. 9), or
of the leper (xiv. 2).   A further group of 13 instances
refers to *torah* in a more general sense, not admitting
of precise identification ; thus, a psalmist says that
God established testimony in Jacob and set *torah* in
Israel (lxxviii. 5).   The remaining 113 examples refer
to the successive codes of written *toroth* (the plural of

[1] Against Begrich, *loc. cit.*, p. 68 ; see S. R. Driver,
Deuteronomy, p 207.
[2] Probably in conscious contrast with the *Torah* of priests and
(popular or cult) prophets.
[3] The sacred lot of Urim and Thummim was no longer
available in post-exilic times.   Cf. Neh. vii. 65 (Ezra ii. 63).

torah) which the Old Testament includes, viz. the
Book of the Covenant, contained in Exod. xx. 22 to
xxiii. 19 (Exod. xxiv. 12, Josh. xxiv. 26), the Deuteronomic Code (Deut. i. 5, 2 Kings xiv. 6, cf. Deut. xxiv.
16; "the roll of the book" in Ps. xl. 8, 9); the
Priestly Code (Neh. viii. 18; cf. Lev. xxiii. 39, and
contrast Deut. xvi. 13), and finally the Pentateuch as
a whole (2 Chron. xxxi. 3, cf. Num. xxviii. 3 ff.;
Ps. i. 2, cxix. 1 ff.). The Rabbinic use of *Torah* to
denote the whole of the Old Testament (Moore,
Judaism, iii, 81; Strack-Billerbeck, i, 671; ii, 542;
iii, 159, 462, 463) naturally lies beyond our scope,
but is illustrated by John x. 34, where Jesus is
represented as introducing a quotation of Ps. lxxxii. 6
by the words, "Is it not written in your law?"
Torah has come to mean "revelation"; as Moore
rightly says, "This is the nearest equivalent to the
Jewish conception of Torah." [1]

2. *The Origins and Sources of Law*

Our survey of the use of the term *torah* has already
reminded us of the variety and wide range of the
origins of Hebrew law, in the sense of direction or
instruction. It can be mediated by priest, judge, and
prophet, the judge denoting the king or a lay elder.
This partly lay origin of law is brought out particularly when we glance at the word which is next in
importance to *torah* for our purpose, viz. *mishpaṭ*.
Properly and originally, this denotes the decision of a
judge (*shopheṭ*). Thus a king of Israel gives a *mishpaṭ*
on an alleged dispute concerning a deposit (1 Kings
xx. 40). Such judgments would often become

[1] *Judaism*, i. 248 n.

precedents for other judgments, and so we have a
collection of them in the *Book of the Covenant* (Exod.
xxi. 1 ff., cf. *v.* 31). These form what we should call
case-law ; they have grown up from time to time as
occasion demanded, e.g. the injury to another man's
ox or ass occasioned by a pit left uncovered. Many
of these " cases " demonstrably go back a millennium
or more to the Code of Hammurabi,[1] and we may
reasonably suppose that they had become the common
usage in Canaan, through the widespread influence of
the Babylonian Code, long before the Israelites
entered it. Agricultural lore is expressly ascribed to
divine " teaching " (the same root as in the term
torah) in Is. xxviii. 26. No inconsiderable part of
Israel's law, in the sense we should distinguish as
secular, sprang from these lay origins.[2] We have an
interesting example of the way in which case-law
could be taken up later into a code, from the decision
made by David as to the distribution of spoil between
combatants and non-combatants (1 Sam. xxx. 24).
It became, we are told, a *mishpaṭ* for Israel from that
day forward, and eventually we find it reappearing
in the Priestly Code (Num. xxxi. 27) as an alleged
part of the Mosaic legislation. The lay legislation of
the elders and other judges must therefore be added
to the *mishpaṭim* obtained by the priestly oracle
(Num. xxvii. 21) when we consider the origins of
Israelite law, whilst the latter part of the Book of
Ezekiel shows how a prophet who was also a priest

---

[1] [On the Code of Hammurabi, see Introductory Lecture by
Professor Murphy on *Primitive Origins of Law in Relation to Religion*,
and the detailed treatment in Dr. Fish's lecture on *Law and
Religion in Babylonia and Assyria*, pp. 36 ff.—ED.]

[2] Cf. Alt, *Die Ursprünge des israelitischen Rechts*, p. 16.

could add to the body of *toroth* (e.g. Ezek. xliii. 12) on lines precisely similar to those of the later Priestly Code. These laws of Ezekiel, as Professor G. A. Cooke reminds us (*Ezekiel*, p. 426), show in phraseology and general aim " how the Priestly Code was beginning to take shape before it arrived at a recognized, official form in the 4th cent."

The precise relation of Ezra to the Torah is a difficult and disputed question. Critical scholarship tends to place him *after* Nehemiah (*c.* 397 B.C.),[1] and to regard his law-book brought from Babylon as either Deuteronomy[2] or (as seems much more probable to the present writer) the Priestly Code, afterwards incorporated into the Pentateuch. His activity would then constitute the *terminus ad quem* of substantial additions to the written Torah. Subsequently to Ezra began that process[3] of the re-adaptation of ancient law to contemporary needs which emerges in the oral tradition of the Pharisees, and was finally crystallized into the Mishnah (A.D. 200), to begin another process of re-interpretation recorded in the Gemara of the Talmud. The consideration of these later developments belongs to subsequent lectures of this series.

How does the fact of this long process of development in the composition of the Pentateuch affect our

---

[1] The reasons are given in my *History of Israel*, chap. vii. § 2.

[2] So L. E. Browne, *Early Judaism*, chap. x.

[3] [This activity can be understood only on the assumption that, no matter which portion of the Pentateuch Ezra read to the assembled people, it is Ezra himself who laid the foundation of subsequent Judaism. It is decisive that he, backed by Persian authority and power, declared the Torah the binding constitution of the Jewish Commonwealth. See also Dr. Herford's *The Law and Pharisaism*, below, p. 93 ff.—ED.]

interpretation of Israel's claim that all its legislation
has its sourcc in God ? It is useful to distinguish these
various *origins* from the one alleged *source*. So far as
origins go (the actual beginnings in history), we cannot
remove the literature and history of Israel from those
of other nations, amongst whom we should find
parallels to most of the features already indicated.
That fact alone is sufficient to remind us that the claim
that a divine revelation has been made to Israel cannot
be based on the particular *means* of mediation. Even
if we were to take certain uncritical and unhistorical
views in later Judaism, and ascribe all legislation
to Moses,[1] we should still be left with the parallel
of the Koran and the claim of Muhammad to be
the prophet of the only true God. To justify the
claim that the Old Testament is indeed the record
of divine revelation, we must establish a philosophy
of revelation deep enough and broad enough to look
beyond all the varied human means and agencies
belonging to these *origins*, and gather them all
under the authority and control of the one source,
God.[2]

The Wisdom of Israel, its nearest approach to
philosophic speculation, gives us some suggestive hints
of what such a philosophy would be. At the close of
our period, we find ben Sira (Eccles. xxiv. 23) identi-
fying Wisdom with the Torah. In Prov. viii. 15, the
personified Wisdom, which is God's master-workman,
declares : " By me kings reign, and princes decree

---

[1] [There are a large number of laws attributed to the Rabbis
(*de-rabbanan*) in contradistinction to the Torah (*de-oraita*).—ED.]

[2] I have treated this subject more fully in my essay " The
Philosophy of Revelation " in the volume called *Record and
Revelation*, edited by me.

justice," [1] whilst another saying of the wise is " The lot is cast into the lap ; but the whole decision thereof is of Yahweh " (Prov. xvi. 33, cf. Is. xxxiv. 17). Thus both the decree of a just judge and what *we* might call the chance decision of the sacred lot are brought under the aegis of divine revelation. The human happening is transformed into a divine event, much as when Joseph looks back on the treachery of his brothers which brought him to Egypt, and declares, " It was not you that sent me hither, but God " (Gen. xlv. 8). These transformations of meaning, wrought by the divine providence, are essential to the Biblical doctrine of God. But they depend on the religious attitude of those concerned, and their conscious acceptance of God's purpose. Moreover, we should most of us hesitate to say that whatever is, is right, or to connect God's will directly with, say, the casting of lots. The prophet Jeremiah was lifting revelation to a new level when he contrasted the prophets he called false with those who really stood in the council of God : " The prophet that hath a dream, let him tell a dream ; and he that hath my word, let him speak my word faithfully " (xxiii. 28).[2]

The ultimate authority of divine law rests in God alone, and not in the particular means which His providence employs to make it known. But this implies, on the human side, that the authority lies in

---

[1] Throughout the monarchical period, we have to remember that the divine kingship is represented by the Davidic kingship. The king's person is sacred ; he is Yahweh's anointed (1 Sam. xxvi. 9) having authoritative knowledge (2 Sam. xiv. 20, xix. 27). This endowment passes eventually to the King-Messiah (Is. xi. 1 ff.).

[2] Cf. also Deut. xiii. 5 and xviii. 15–22 on true and false prophets.

the quality of what is revealed, its intrinsic worth.[1]
It is again Jeremiah who gives us the surest clue to
this, when he reports God as saying to him : " If thou
wilt take the precious from the common, thou shalt
be as my mouth " (xv. 19). Tradition always goes
back to some kind of value-judgment.

3. *Law and Ideal*

If we are to grasp the full significance of law for
religion, we must contrast it with the other great way
of controlling human conduct, viz. that of the ideal.
For this the Greeks are the pioneers and exemplars.
The model man, for Aristotle, has his resources
within himself. The typical Greek virtues, wisdom,
courage, temperance, justice, are all conceived as
expressions of the due proportions and harmony of a
human life, and have little to do with the conventional
gods, who are far from being " virtuous " in this sense.
We have only to think of the Old Testament summary
of man's duty to see the difference between the kind
of life based on human ideal and that based on divine
law : " What doth Yahweh require of thee, but to do
justice and to love mercy, and to walk humbly with
thy God ? " (Micah vi. 8). This difference is partly
due to the fact that Greek individualism developed
outside the state, with its traditional religion, and
struggled, as we saw at the outset, towards a better
type of religion, whereas Hebrew individualism always
developed *within* the consciousness of community
linked to God. Consequently, the Greek thinker
moved towards the conception of a law of nature,

[1] Thus Spiritualism is condemned by the poor content of its
" revelations," for which no abnormality of *means* can give
authority.

whereas the Hebrew believer ascribed all the laws of conduct to divine revelation. The Greek moves from below upwards, the Hebrew from above downwards. Doubtless there is much common ground where they meet, but even this will have a different aspect because of the different approach to it. We must not forget that Greek thought at its highest climbed to a genuine relation to God and the unseen ; we have only to think of the closing paragraph of the ninth book of the *Republic* : " perhaps in heaven there is laid up the pattern of it (the ideal city) for him who wishes to behold it, and beholding, to found a city in himself." We have also to remember Plato's assumption of a revelation given to the soul in its pre-existent state, towards the recovery of which it strives on earth—an assumption based on a psychological dichotomy which has no parallel in Hebrew thought. The very term " ideal " is derived from the Platonic concept of the " idea," to denote the true nature or essence of a thing, with all the religious potentialities of Plato's use of the concept.

On the other hand, the Greek development shows the tendency of the ideal to produce a philosophy rather than a religion. The ideal is likely to be wider in scope than the commanded law, and less anchored to the customs of a particular generation ; but what it gains in extensity it loses in intensity. The philosophical morality of the Stoic came to an end, because it lacked that religious foundation possessed by the morality of both Judaism and Christianity.

Even from a purely pedagogic standpoint, law is necessary. Moral law in relation to conduct holds the same place as creed in relation to religious faith. Each forms an anatomy rather than a physiology.

Much beside law is needed to create the good life, and much beyond creed to create the life of faith. But, though we refuse to believe with Housman that " every mother's son travails with a skeleton " as his final output, he does need a skeleton as the framework of his present activity. Law is necessary in education, though education points beyond law. The point is admirably expressed in an early book written by the Archbishop of York : [1] he describes the process by which the child is made to attend, i.e. to practise concentration on lessons, the matter of which is of very secondary importance ; the discipline is the important thing, and continues through the school life until " the educator may say, I have created a will in you ; at first you were a mere mass of impulses ; I have co-ordinated and systematized those impulses so that now you have a real will and purpose of your own ; I have forced you into freedom ; now go and exercise that freedom." So we may say of Israel, with Köhler,[2] that God's first act of grace to man was the giving of a command.

4. The Adequacy of Israel's Law

If we grant the pedagogic necessity for law in religion, what of the adequacy of the divine commandments actually found in Israel's religion ? How far can the laws of the Pentateuch be justified as divine revelation, i.e. as possessing the permanent value and applicability which is claimed for them by Judaism ? [3]

---

[1] Temple, *Nature of Personality*, pp. 28–29.

[2] *Theologie des Alten Testaments*, p. 189.

[3] Cf. H. Loewe in *Judaism and Christianity*, i. 177 : " Torah cannot be abrogated : when it has permeated the hearts of all men, its outward symbols will cease automatically."

Certain features only of this question can come into review, and only those which properly attach to the Old Testament period ; there can be no question here of any attempt to weigh the merits or demerits of the later Judaism, or the larger question of the universal claims of " Torah " (Is. ii. 2 ff. = Mic. iv. 1 ff.).

In the first place, the very differences in the successive codes of law in the Pentateuch remind us that just so far as law is precisely applicable to one age or generation, it ceases to be directly applicable to another, exhibiting a different type of society and different social or religious customs.[1] To take a single example, the Book of the Covenant (Exod. xx. 24) commands a plurality of altars, whilst the Deuteronomic Code enacts that the altar at Jerusalem shall be the only one (Deut. xii). Changing needs always require some method of bringing particular laws up to date. When once the law has been fixed as divinely authorized, the simplest way of making it applicable for a later generation with new circumstances is the unwritten law of interpretation, which has been used so widely in Judaism, Islam and Christianity. Strictly speaking, this method is a legal fiction, just as much as is the legal ruling on some fresh set of circumstances given by a judge to-day, which is avowedly based on the precedents of the past, though actually it goes beyond them and so makes new law.

In the second place, it is clear that law in the sense of precise rules, positive or negative, does not necessarily affect the inner life at all. That is illustrated

[1] [See on this question A. Menes, " Die vorexilischen Gesetze Israels," *Beiheft* 50 d. *Zeitschrift f. alttest. Wissenschaft.—* ED.]

in modern secular legislation, which takes account of a man's actions, but not of his thoughts when they do not become overt in action. Any religion, therefore, which emphasizes law is in danger of what is called "legalism," just as a religion which shuns law is in danger of "antinomianism," with its emotional perils. But the religion of Israel, as it is developed in the Old Testament, is very far from being a legalistic religion, in the dyslogistic sense. Lord Macmillan, writing on "Law and Religion," says of the Old Testament that "the whole conception of the relationship between God and man is legal." [1] His misconception is due to his taking "covenant" to mean "contract," which is a very misleading rendering of the Hebrew term, *berith*. It would be much truer to say that *berith* is the external expression of one of the richest religious words in the Old Testament, viz. *ḥeśed*, which we know as "loving-kindness," though it includes the sense of loyalty as well as of love. *Berith* is the shell, and *ḥeśed* is the kernel. No mere "legalism" could have inspired the 119th Psalm or such a couplet as Ps. xl. 8 :

> "I delight to do thy will, O my God,
> Yea, thy Torah is within my heart.[2]"

The fact is that *torah*, as we have seen, meant much more than "law." It included all the truths of God's providence and redemptive activity which are illustrated in the Pentateuch, as well as elsewhere in the Old Testament. This is why the prophet Jeremiah can think of a new *berith* with Israel, in which God's *torah* shall be written on the hearts of Israelites, and

[1] *Law and Other Things*, p. 64.
[2] Lit. "bowels," the seat of affection. Cf. Song of Songs, v. 4.

become an inner motive. This, too, is why we meet
with the paradox that would startle us if it were not
so familiar—" Thou shalt love the Lord thy God."
How can love be commanded ? It cannot—but, as
the sixth chapter of Deuteronomy goes on to show, the
God who commands love has shown Himself to be a
lovable God. The answer to the question, " What
mean the testimonies and the statutes and the judgments which the Lord our God hath commanded
you ? " is " We were Pharaoh's bondmen in Egypt ;
and the Lord brought us out of Egypt with a mighty
hand." The God of Israel is a redemptive God, and
therefore a God to be loved, who *is* loved when once
He is known in His mighty acts. Along this line of
thought, therefore, it becomes wholly credible that
zeal for the Torah could inspire the Maccabean
Revolt, and so much else in Jewish history, which
" legalism " would never explain.

In the third place, we have to notice that mingling
of ritual and moral elements in the Jewish law which
seems to make them of equal importance. Here it is
better that a Jewish voice should speak. Mr. C. G.
Montefiore,[1] in his *Hibbert Lectures* (p. 178), says,
" the drawback or misfortune of such a code was its
equal accentuation of the ceremonial and the moral.
More precisely, the evil lay in that mournful relic of
outworn paganism—the conception of external holi-
ness and pollution, of clean and unclean. The law
was far less a misfortune in virtue of its legalism than
because of its heterogeneous contents." This ought
to be frankly admitted, even whilst we remember that
the soul of religion always needs a body, and that

[1] It should be understood that he represents " liberal " and
not " orthodox " Judaism.

even survival-practices may be charged with sacramental meaning for the devout mind.[1]

The fourth point calling for notice here is that of the influence of the whole conception of God as lawgiver, and consequently as judge. Admittedly, that is not the only or even the primary conception of God in the Old Testament : we have only to read the 103rd Psalm to learn that. Authority belongs to fatherhood as well as to kingship, however loose the conception of parental authority in modern days. But there is an issue deeper than this. How far, and in what way, does law adequately reflect or express the nature of God ? Is the law simply the expression of His arbitrary will, or does He Himself obey a law of righteousness conceived to exist outside Himself? Such questions have occupied considerable space in Christian theology, and apparently are not unknown to Jewish thought, in view of the claim that the law existed before the creation of the world.[2] We shall perhaps come as near to the truth as our mortal speech can, if we say with Dale [3] : " The relation between God and the eternal Law of Righteousness is . . . unique. He is not, as we are, bound by its authority ; in Him its authority is actively asserted. . . . In God the law is *alive* : it reigns on His throne, sways His sceptre, is crowned with His glory." I imagine that a Jew as well as a Christian could accept such a statement.

---

[1] I was once sitting next to a Jewish Rabbi, when something had been said about " mere ritualism." With evidently deep emotion he said, " When I bind on my phylacteries for morning prayer, it is not for me ' mere ritualism.' "

[2] Moore, *op. cit.*, i. 266 ff.

[3] *The Atonement*, ed. 13, p. 372.

5. *Law in Relation to the Revelation in History*

In what has been said about the necessary limitations of law as given to a particular generation or people, in terms comprehensible by it, we have had before us a particular case of the problem of historical revelation in general, which every religion based on history must face, in one form or another. If God is to enter history, He must accept those conditions of history which have arisen through His creative purpose. He must take up the temporal into the eternal, that the eternal may be intelligible. The living God is not the God of a single generation, yet He must speak in the language of each generation to which He would draw near. From this point of view, the largest and fullest revelation of the eternal which can be given in time is but a fragment of the whole that God has to give. The value of that which is given is not to be measured simply by what it is, but by what it does. In choosing law as one of the ways of His revelation, God has given us not an end in itself but a means to an end, a human symbol of divine purpose, which is also an instrument of that purpose. Jew and Christian are one in believing that the supreme goal is the satisfying " knowledge " of God, a knowledge not of the intellect alone, but actualized in the obedient will. Both Jew and Christian can say, " In His will is our peace." Both the religion of the Law and the religion of the Gospel draw from the deep wells of the revelation of God in history.[1]

[1] This theme is further developed in my essay " The Philosophy of Revelation," in the volume *Record and Revelation* (Clarendon Press).

F

SELECT BIBLIOGRAPHY TO LECTURE III, "LAW AND
RELIGION IN ISRAEL"

DRIVER, S. R. : Article "Law (in Old Testament)," *Hastings's Dictionary of the Bible*, vol. iii (1900).

BENZINGER, I. : Article "Law and Justice," *Encyclopædia Biblica*, vol. iii (1902).

KENT, C. F. : *Israel's Laws and Legal Precedents* (1907).

KÜCHLER, F. : "Das priesterliche Orakel in Israel und Juda," *B.Z.A.W.* 33 (1918).

GRAY, G. BUCHANAN : *Sacrifice in the Old Testament* (The Hebrew Priesthood) (1925).

PEDERSEN, JOHS. : *Israel, its Life and Culture* (1926).

MOORE, G. F. : *Judaism* (1927).

JIRKU, A. . *Das weltliche Recht im Alten Testament* (1927).

MENES, A. : (1) "Die vorexilischen Gesetze Israels," *B.Z.A.W.* 50 (1928).

(2) Article "Gesetze" I, in *Enc. Jud.* viii.

HEMPEL, J. : Article "Recht und Religion" in ed. 2 of *Die Religion in Geschichte und Gegenwart* (1930).

SMITH, J. M. P. : *The Origin and History of Hebrew Law* (1931).

ALT, A. : *Die Ursprünge des israelitischen Rechts* (1934).

BEGRICH, J. : "Die priesterliche Tora," *B.Z.A.W.* 66 (1936).

WELCH, A. C. : *Prophet and Priest in Old Israel* (1936).

MONTEFIORE, C. G. : "The Old Testament and Judaism," in *Record and Revelation*, ed. by H. Wheeler Robinson (1938).

[*B.Z.A.W.* = "Beiheft of the Zeitschrift für die alttestamentliche Wissenschaft."]

IV

LAW AND RELIGION AMONGST THE SAMARITANS

BY

EDWARD ROBERTSON

IV

THE origins of many human institutions are lost in the mists of antiquity, and where man has no certain tradition of origin he ascribes it to a god. According to a legend of the seafaring Phœnicians navigation had its earliest beginning when the god Thoth put to sea on a log. The origin of writing is another case in point. Man cannot recall a time when he was without it. It must consequently be of divine origin. In Babylonia its invention was attributed to Ea, Nabu or Marduk, in Egypt to Thoth, in Greece to Hermes or Prometheus, in the Norse lands to Odin. According to Jewish tradition, Enoch, Abraham or Moses was the first to make use of writing, but to the Samaritans the Torah was written by the very finger of God Himself.

It is not surprising that law should be, in respect of antiquity of origin, in the same category as writing. The incidence of law on human society reaches so far back in history—in fact beyond written history—that a human origin for it was precluded in popular belief. It was commonly accepted by early peoples that it could only have come from heaven for the benefit of man. It was so amongst the ancient Egyptians, and it was so in Babylonia. Everyone is familiar with the stele on which are inscribed the laws associated with the name of Hammurabi. On its upper part is a

representation of the Babylonian king in the presence
of the Sun-god, the suggestion being that he received
his law code, presumably by dictation, from Shamash
himself. So it was also in later times with the Greeks
and the Romans. Both Demosthenes and Cicero felt
impelled to proclaim that law was a gift from the
gods to man. Here, too, Hebrew traditions and
beliefs are in accord. Their Law was to the Hebrews
a divine institution, communicated to Moses by God
on Mt. Sinai.

To the modern critic such simple belief and explanation is clear evidence of the great age of the institution
and its supreme value, but it suggests to him also a
convenient way of shelving the obscure problem of
origin. He himself sees in law a long process of
evolution whose rudiments were based on tribal
custom. It is of the very essence of law that it should
be backed by an authority which will ensure and, if
needs be, enforce its observance. There is implicit in
every law a penalty, and law cannot become effective,
is in fact not law but mere demand or assertion, unless
the penalty can be exacted when occasion demands.
Whilst the attribution of divine origin to the art
of writing might be to man only idle speculation
or the easy satisfaction of intellectual curiosity, the
case of law was in a different category. Power is a
main attribute of deity, and if law were recognized as
of divine origin, the authority which law required for
its successful operation was now transferred from the
family, tribe or nation to deity. The divine power
now operating behind law and enforcing it was invisible and intangible but none the less real and
effective in the hold it had on men's minds and the
control it exercised on their lives. Man is generally

more afraid of the unseen terror than of the seen. We are thus made witnesses of law starting on earth as tribal regulation, being transferred to heaven by human consent, and returning to earth again as revelation backed by all the tremendous power of its sponsor deity.

It must not be supposed that law, or a law code, could be transferred in a single act in a single moment of time from earth to heaven in order to descend again with a new-found authority greatly in excess of the original. In early times man's daily life was never distinguished from his religious. The two were always merged, and the regulations he evolved to control communal life were never devoid of a supernatural element. The sense of equity, too, on which all law ultimately bases, beyond cavil innate in mankind, was itself recognized as a divine gift to man. It made no difference whether the belief of the people was in henotheism or monotheism. Where the writ of the god ran there his law was enforceable, for in him resided the might and the means to insist on its fulfilment.

Such may be presumed to have been the early history of the Torah, but whilst the legal portion can be recognized as its kernel, it had attracted to it in its early state traditions and commentary, the whole forming a body of scriptures. The sanctification of scriptures is a slow-moving but intensely interesting process. Not only must they be concerned with deity and man's relationship to him, but they must be hallowed by time. All trace of human authorship must be given time to disappear and be forgotten, whilst the contents come to be regarded with an ever-growing and ever-deepening veneration. From that

stage to an assertion and recognition of divine authorship is but a step, especially in a community with a
belief in the direct intervention of deity in the earth
process and his participation in the affairs of men.
All this lies behind us in the history of the Torah.

The law code of the Jews and Samaritans is found
embedded in the Pentateuch. To them the Pentateuch is the Torah or teaching of God. That the
Torah is revelation is for both an article of faith and
not a subject of conjecture or of historical investigation.
Both believe it was communicated to Israel through
the great prophet and lawgiver, Moses. In later
times, when they had an opportunity to put on record
their religious speculations, both postulated for the
Torah a separate pre-existence. While both accept it
as divinely revealed and find in its teaching their rule
of life, they are not one in their attitude towards it, nor
yet one in their interpretation of it. Their exemplars
of the Torah vary slightly in text in a few passages
which, however, are vital to their beliefs and have
sent them to travel different roads. The crux of their
dispute is the location of the " place which God chose
to put his name there." To the Jews the place was
Jerusalem : to the Samaritans, Mt. Gerizim. Over
it they have quarrelled and history can surely never
have known another feud so bitter, so lasting and so
apparently irreconcilable. Their common possession
of the Torah, which might be expected to unite them
closely, separates them. Each party appeals to its
text for confirmation and the text of each justifies the
trust placed in it. One or other has falsified the
original text. But which ?

The origin of the Samaritans as a religious body is
a controversial subject. Most modern investigators

see in the Samaritans only a semi-Jewish sect which
first appeared on the stage of history at the Return
under Ezra, when their proffered co-operation in re-
building the Temple was declined. They were
fortunate in finding as leader and High Priest
Manasseh, a grandson of Eliashub, the Jewish High
Priest, who had contracted one of the mixed marriages
denounced by Nehemiah, but having as his father-in-
law Sanballat the Horonite. He was " chased " from
Jerusalem, but took with him a copy of the Law and
ministered on Mt. Gerizim in a temple erected for
him by Sanballat. Dr. Gaster, himself a Jew, has
repeatedly attacked this view. He shows con-
vincingly that the Samaritans must have existed as
a religious community long before that time and,
moreover, had possession also of their Torah. On
what grounds, he asks, could they have made over-
tures to Zerubbabel but on the basis of the possession
of the same religious teaching as the Jews ? His
reading of Ezra is that the Samaritans, who claim to
be the direct descendants of the Israelite inhabitants
of the Northern Kingdom, invited the returning Jews
to recognize their temple on Mt. Gerizim as the true
place of worship selected by God and to unite with
them in common worship there. This the Jews
rejected. The contention that the " Cuthæans "
accepted priest, scriptures, and temple at the hands
of the Jews and blossomed in a night into the Samaritan community, is almost incredible. Gaster would
seem to be right in maintaining that the body of
Jewish traditions was taking shape long before Ezra,
and that too much is ascribed by the Jews to him, and
by modern critics to the men of the Great Synagogue.
The Samaritans looked upon the temple founded by

Eli at Shiloh as schismatic and that at Jerusalem as heretical. That they could ever have taken over a copy of the teaching prepared by one whom they called the " cursed Ezra," surpasses belief. The very fact that they possess the Torah written in the ancient Hebrew script—almost identical with that found recently on the Lachish potsherds, dating from the time of Jeremiah—is a strong argument on the Samaritan side.

In treating of the association, or rather perhaps the dissociation, of Jews and Samaritans, the question of the time in history when the Torah was accepted by the Hebrews as divine revelation does not concern us here. It was at least antecedent to the commencement of the great feud. The Jews maintained that Moses wrote down the Law to God's dictation. The Samaritans believed that the Torah was written by the finger of God and then given to Moses to copy.[1] From him it was passed on to the priests and the elders. To believe that the Law was written by God's very hand does not leave any loophole for human frailties. There can be no scribal errors, no superfluities. Every word and letter must have significance, and all knowledge for all living is present in its text if its pages are rightly interpreted. But although we are not directly concerned with the time of the origin of the Law, we are much concerned with its later history.

A body of teaching accepted as divine revelation, although it is endued with all the might and majesty which attaches necessarily to it, is not without draw-

---

[1] A later view given in the *Molad Mosheh* of Ishmael Rumaihi (sixteenth century) was that the Most High recited it to the Glory (*Kabod*) and the Glory recited it to Moses.

backs in a community whose social life gradually changes and becomes more complex in the course of time. Originally fashioned in and for a relatively simple society, the problem of adjusting its teaching and especially its legislative provisions to altered conditions is obviously not an easy one. Nothing contained in the document can be abrogated, nothing suppressed, nothing altered. This in time became the problem of Jews and Samaritans in respect of the Law. The Law was not comprehensive enough in its legislation nor explicit enough in its presentation. Thus it said that no work was to be done on the Sabbath day, but gave no definition of work. It made a number of religious services obligatory, but gave no complete ritual for their proper observance. It was left to man to deduce from the Law how these and other requirements were to be met. Close searching of the text and appropriate exegesis might be expected to fill many a gap. An enlargement of the Law in the belief of the Jew was provided for him by special messages from God who spake through prophets, but such messages required certification, and after a time they too ceased, or at least were no longer accepted. But many of these writings, which were spread over several centuries, attached themselves as a fringe to the Law. Eventually the canon of Scripture was closed, and for a period of over a century no additional scriptural writing appeared amongst the Jews, but all the while there was in process an oral interpretation and supplementing of the Torah later to have the name of Moses attached to it, and be given an authority not far short of that of the Torah itself. Thus were the Jews enabled to interpret the divine will with the aid of a greatly extended Law.

But with the Samaritans it was different.   They
acccpted thc Law but would admit no other writings
as Holy Scriptures.   Their aim was to keep the letter
of the Law, and they prided themselves on their name,
which they aver has no connexion with Samaria.
They are *Shomerim*—that is, " keepers " of the Law
of God.   Obviously one way of meeting the requirements of the Law is to mould life to conform to its
narrow compass.   And this to a marked degree was
the solution of the problem which commended itself
to the Samaritans.   In so doing they but trod the
path of most literalists.   Christianity, especially early
Christianity, was never without its monasteries and its
anchorites.   This preservation of their lives on the
plane of rigour and simplicity in conformity with the
literal interpretation of the Law was the more
feasible for the Samaritans since, although they were
numerous until the persecutions of Jewish and Christian rulers of Palestine reduced their numbers, they
were never in any great numbers scattered abroad.
The Jews had to face a very different and much more
difficult situation.   They were dispersed abroad from
the days of the Exile in many lands and were faced at
every turn with the problem of adjusting their lives to
new and complex social orders.   They could not
ignore the strain put upon them by the new conditions.
Their very existence often depended upon their
successfully adapting themselves to their new sur-
roundings.   The plain Jew could not be expected to
understand just where he stood religiously in all
circumstances and in how far the Law permitted him
to compromise.   He had to appeal to the learned in
the Law for guidance, and as the mantle of the Law
was spread ever wider and wider, a vast Talmudic

literature supplied interpretation and direction. It must not be supposed that the Samaritans remained entirely unaffected. In the pursuit of their polemics they kept in touch with Jewish methods of interpretation of the Law and Jewish literature. There is evidence of imitation of the Jewish lead in all phases of Biblical literature, except, of course, in the non-Pentateuchal canonical writings, and always where dates can be determined the Samaritans, as might be expected, are found to lag behind the Jews. Samaritan literature as now known is not very extensive. It is a Samaritan boast that at one time they were possessed of many books and a wide range of literature which were destroyed by the Emperor Hadrian. Of the early stage of the supplementary literature to the Torah they have the *Hillukh* and the *Kitab al-Tubbakh*, but both in their existing forms of composition are of relatively recent date, although both no doubt incorporate elements of a much earlier period. To correspond to the Jewish oral Law the Samaritans offer the *Kitab al-Asatir*, which, like the Jewish oral Law, is ascribed to Moses. Gaster, who has edited the work, regards it as one of the earliest pieces of Samaritan literature and prior to their Targum. The veneration attaching to it was such that commentaries on its text were composed—a treatment normally reserved for the Holy Scriptures.

Another device of the Jews to overcome their difficulties was to strain the letter of the Law. Thus, in order to circumvent the Sabbath restrictions which pressed heavily upon them in competition with the Gentiles, they invented the *'erub*, a kind of legal fiction. A case in point was the Sabbath day's journey. By placing food for a couple of meals at the limit of a Sabbath day's journey the traveller was permitted to treat that as his home and make it a fresh point of departure. The Samaritans despised such methods and would have nothing to do with '*erubin*.

The Hellenization of the Eastern Mediterranean world affected both Jew and Samaritan. Greek civilization spread everywhere and aroused admiration. Greek customs found ready imitators. Greek philosophy stirred men's minds. Jewry in its high places in due course fell under the spell and appeared heading for disruption and disaster, when it was brought up sharp by the Maccabean Revolt. The Samaritans do not appear to have taken part in either the Hellenic movement or in the Maccabean struggles. The bitter enmity which they cherished against the Jews would not permit them to side with and actively support the Maccabees, and in consequence they suffered when in due time John Hyrcanus wreaked vengeance on them and destroyed their temple.

With the spread of Greek culture came the spread of the Greek language. Written in Hebrew, the Torah was made use of by worshippers using the Aramaic and Greek tongues and, in the case of the Samaritans especially, the Arabic. The need for translations arose. At first the services of an interpreter were used in the synagogues, and in order to make the meaning clear he often had recourse to paraphrase. When written Targums supplanted him, his method and words were embodied in them. The Aramaic paraphrasings are of particular interest, for they show us the trend of Jewish religious thought and speculation under the impact of foreign ideas. When the Palestinian Targum translates Deuteronomy xxx. 20,

" that thou mayest obey His voice and cleave unto
Him : for He is thy life and the length of thy days,"
as " to obey His words and to keep close to His fear,
for the Law in which you occupy yourselves will be
your life in this world and the length of your days in
the world to come," [1] we see the inquiring glance
cast towards a world beyond the grave. Unfortunately
the dates of the Targums cannot be fixed with any
certainty. In the form in which we have them they
may well be and probably are later than the Jewish
apocalyptic literature, but reflected in the Targums
we see the mind of the Jew of the pre-apocalyptic
period at work.

It is not perhaps surprising that the Law when
accepted by Jew and Samaritan as revelation still
displayed many features of its previous terrestrial
existence. As a document sent from heaven and the
fountain of all knowledge for man it might have been
expected to cover man's life from before the cradle
to after the grave. Instead the Law is silent on any
state of pre-existence and vague and unsatisfying on
post-existence. The world lit by the sun and moon
seemed to be all that mattered, and God could execute
all He had planned for man in the short span between
birth and death. The explanation of its failure to deal
with more than the life on earth no doubt lies in the
fact that the main concern of the Torah is the relationship of the people to God rather than that of the
individual ; and the life of a nation is not measured
by the span of human life. But even before the Exile
the religious importance of the individual was being
recognized and stressed, and the problem of the hereafter had begun to obtrude itself on men's minds.

[1] Gaster, *S.O.L.A.T.*, p. 41.

The wider horizon offered to Jewish thought by contact with the philosophies and religions of West and East—a contact made easier by the conquests of Alexander the Great—led eventually to the shaping of an eschatology. Suddenly—so at least it seems—between the second century B.C. and the first century A.D. there appeared a remarkable number of apocalyptic writings. They were the fruit of a tree that appeared to have been growing in secret and maturing in the centuries which preceded. But while the threads of the arguments by which reflective Judaism arrived at its eschatology had to lead back—or rather had to be led back—to its Bible, it could at least, if it so desired, include the prophetical writings as well as the Torah. It was here that the Samaritans were at a disadvantage, for they had only the Torah to which to appeal. This fact emphasizes the dependence of the Samaritans on the Jewish lead, for the eschatology they came to profess, bearing as it does a close resemblance to the Jewish, could hardly have been evolved *ab initio* from the Torah alone. They kept pace, however, with Jewish eschatology by attaching doctrines, often by very thin threads, to the text of the Pentateuch.

The question of the " last things " began to loom large before the Jew of the Hellenic period. He had been thrown earlier into contact with Parseeism, which included the doctrine of the continuance of the soul after death. Platonism with its doctrine of the immortality of the soul contributed its stimulus. The Stoics held that evil souls were punished after death, and Pluto's kingdom had the four judges, Minos, Rhadamanthus, Aeacus and Triptolemos, a belief in which they were followed by the Romans.

The Jews themselves, too, felt the need to bring the end of man's life within the purview of their religion. The doctrine that within the compass of man's short life on earth God would amply reward him for all his righteousness did not appear to be borne out in human experience. The problem is well expressed in the Samaritan *Hillukh*, a work to which we have already referred.

" There are many people who do not keep the commandments of the Lord, and yet have no suffering, no persecution and no punishment, and they are living in this world full of rejoicing and pleasure more than all the faithful ones, and they rule over the faithful ones who keep the Law of God, and perform its commandments and statutes, and if there would be no other world where the man should obtain the reward for his deeds, every man who turns to evil would obtain his desires more than any man who was faithful to the Lord, blessed be He and His Law." It was thus unthinkable that death should end all and God's promises remain unfulfilled. The extension of man's life into the hereafter seemed unavoidable, and an act of judgment to determine reward or punishment essential. In the words of a writer of the last century before the Christian era put in the mouth of a scribe : " For though for the present time I should be delivered from the punishment of men : yet should I not escape the hand of the Almighty, neither alive, nor dead " (2 Macc. vi. 26). Thus as concomitants of the world to come came naturally the immortality of the soul and an act of judgment, or a mass judgment, on a particular day. As an extension of these articles of faith came the belief in the resurrection of the body and the advent of the Messiah.

G

The Samaritans took over most of these doctrines from the Jews, and where necessary re-shaped them to fall within the ambit of their own faith.   Their eschatology eventually included beliefs in the resurrection of the body and the Day of Judgment.   The Samaritan conception of the latter in its earliest form is found in the " Book of Wonders " (*Sefer Pele'athah*) of Marqah, exegete, poet and liturgist.   His date is given by the Samaritans themselves as the first century B.C., but Western critics place him in the fourth century A.D.   According to Marqah [1] the Day of Judgment is a day of vengeance for all sinners and one of recompense for the good and the evil, a day of shaking for all feet and of quivering for all limbs, a day of weeping, a day of resurrection, a day of assembly, a day of truth, a day of dread, a day of unhappiness for all sinners, a day of joy for all obedient, a day on which the Lord of the world reveals Himself and proclaims " I, I am he and there is none other beside me " (Deut. xxxii. 39).   The earth in its terror splits open.   In a moment all is laid bare.   In a moment all stand up, and when the earth opens over the righteous there is emitted a good odour which penetrates to the highest abode.   It is, however, otherwise with the wicked.   From them rises the evil smell of their dust.   The odour of the righteous is acceptable.   Their clothes are new, as is said of them, " Your clothing shall not grow old upon you " (Deut. xxix. 5).   Adam and Noah and the righteous of the world stand before them, and the angels of His good pleasure surround them.   Moses is glad with them, and Aaron rejoices on their account. There is a happy gathering in which also Eleazar,

[1] See Heidenheim, *Bibliotheca Samaritana*, iii. 143 f.

Phinehas, Joshua, Caleb and the Seventy Elders take part, singing praises. The fate of the sinners who stand over against them is, however, far from happy. Their evil odour rises from the earth and is mixed with fire and brimstone. They appear with bodies blackened, with clothes rent and faces troubled. Of them it is said, " Wherefore look ye so sadly today ? " (Gen. xl. 7). Cain, Lamech, the people of the Flood, the people of Sodom, the people of Babel, the Egyptians, the Amalekites, Korah and his associates all smite them with their hands. The Angels of Wrath beset them, dust and ashes rain down upon them. Their eyes are downcast. Moses and Aaron evince their displeasure. The Great Fire sears their bodies, and God pities them not.

The foregoing is interesting as showing how anxious the Samaritans were to link their eschatological conceptions with the text of the Torah. As will be seen, none of the Jewish apocalypses which bring into their theme the Day of Judgment is the immediate progenitor of the Samaritan, although there are some common elements with the Book of Jubilees.

The Samaritans saw beyond the resurrection of the body at the Day of Judgment a transformed earthly kingdom based on Mt. Gerizim. According to the *Kitab al-Tabbakh*, a Samaritan work of the Arabic period but containing earlier elements, the two worlds cannot exist together at one and the same time. One vanishes as the other appears. Creatures are brought to life again and the idols vanish. In this present world people who pray for the intercession of the holy prophets may expect benefit, but no prayers are accepted in the world to come. The new world appears to be the old world purified, for it is pointed out that as soon as the earth is no longer contaminated with the bones of the dead it will be ritually pure. In the poetic picture of Abisha b. Phinehas (*d.* 1378), at the Day of Vengeance all will be destroyed save the everlasting hill (Gerizim) and the Garden of Eden. When the dead rise each one is asked what he did in the flesh and is confronted with the Torah. Those who can obtain no support from the three meritorious ones will weep tears of blood. The people are then marshalled in two divisions. The division of the righteous passes on to the Garden of Eden, whilst the sinners are burned in the fire like incense.

In this second world or kingdom the Samaritans postulated a ruler, the *Taheb* or "Restorer." The idea seems to have been borrowed from the Jewish Messiah. Obviously the Samaritans could not model their *Taheb* strictly on the Jewish pattern. A Messiah of the line of David ruling in a sanctified land but with Jerusalem as capital was to them anathema. Their *Taheb* would rule but he would rule the new kingdom with Gerizim as centre. In the earliest form of the conception they identified the *Taheb* with Joseph, whose bones had been brought from Egypt by the Children of Israel for burial near the foot of Mt. Gerizim. The name of Joshua, too, was thought of in this connexion. As time passed and the second kingdom became more and more transcendent, Moses became the ideal *Taheb*. It was fitting that he who acted as intermediary between God and man in this world should again be the leader in the world to come. His appearance, said the Samaritans of the Muslim occupation of Palestine, will herald the abandonment of the Arabic tongue in favour of the divine Hebrew. The world will turn to belief in one God and will

seek the shadow of His house on Mt. Gerizim, the
gate of heaven, and will trust in Moses and his
teaching.   Then they cannot forbear adding, " But
cursed be Ezra and his words which in his wickedness
he wrote."

With the Muslim conquest of Palestine the Samaritan community became a small island in the midst of
a great sea.   And just as they were influenced by
Judaistic beliefs, so in time they were affected by
Islam.   No alteration was made in the fundamentals
of their faith, but it is interesting to see that when they
began to write their books in Arabic, probably from
about the ninth century onwards, they headed them
with the customary Arabic ascriptional phrases.   They
even translated these back into Samaritan for use
in works written in Samaritan.   They modelled their
Arabic literary style on the *maqamah*, and their hymns
and other poems reflected Arabic metrical form
rather than the rhythmic measures of the Jews.

The provinces of divine and human law, while they
to a certain extent overlap, vary in extent and
character.   Divine law operates also in the domain of
morals, which human law would rather exclude from
its purview.   Thus our criminal law is interested in
motive only as a factor in promoting crime.   Divine
law is concerned with the regulation of all motive and
the repression of all wrong impulse, independent of
their expression in crime.   Divine law or revelation,
whilst it gains enormously in the authoritative hold
it exercises on men's minds, suffers from the disability
of its consequent changeless fixity.   Human law is
elastic and its authority varies with the effectiveness
of the human power behind it.   Evaders of its provisions may successfully elude punishment, for those

who administer it may be deceived. In the case of
divine law there can be no evasion, for God is not
mocked. It did appear at one time to the Jews, and
also to the Samaritans, that death was providing a
means of escape for the wicked from the punishment
they had earned, and the Law was silent on their fate.
But, as we have seen, by means of an eschatology
threaded on to their Bible in the case of the Jews and
pinned on to the Torah in the case of the Samaritans,
the wicked were caught in a safe net and divine law
was finally vindicated.

The need to use the Law as an oracle to speak the
fateful word has never ceased. Round the Law as
nucleus fringe after fringe of interpretative literature
has been draped. No other body of literature has ever
been subjected to such close scrutiny and such variety
of interpretation as the Law. Typology, allegory,
mysticism, symbolism, Gematria, have all made the
Torah speak in their name for Jewish interpreters ;
and, as we have had occasion to note, the chief
interpretative and speculative systems of the Jews
have been later adopted by the Samaritans. Take
allegory as another case in point. Allegorism was
found to be a useful means of squaring the vulnerable
tenets of unshakable faith with the destructive arguments of implacable reason, without repudiating
either. Greek philosophers had found it convenient to
allegorize Homer. Allegorical interpretation of the
Law was introduced by Jewish philosophers, since it
left them free to indulge to the full their philosophical
speculations without running counter to it. In the
first century Philo could reconcile the Torah with
Platonic philosophy by the aid of allegory. By the
beginning of the second century even such conservative

leaders of schools as Rabbi Ishmael and Rabbi Aqibah were seeking an occasional and hesitating refuge in allegory. By the fourth century we find it in the exegesis of the Samaritan Marqah along with symbolism expressed through Gematria. It seems idle to postulate a spreading of the mantle of the Law by the Samaritans parallel to, and independent of, that of the Jews. The Jewish developments were mainly the product of the special circumstances of the Diaspora and the incidence of forces whose working can often be traced. Such were not paralleled in the situation of the Samaritans. The Samaritan acceptance of the Jewish lead in spite of their mutual hostility is a supreme tribute to the value of the Jewish solutions of their eternal problem, how to get God to pronounce on every problem of human life and conduct through His Scriptures. Throughout the long course of their history the Samaritans have clung tenaciously to their Law and denied validity to any supplementary Scriptures, but clearly they have not disdained to adopt and adapt means of widening its scope without altering its letter. In this obviously they have not been leaders, nor probably even collaborators, but have followed the Jews afar off.

LITERATURE

CHARLES, R. H. : *The Apocrypha and Pseudepigrapha of the Old Testament* (Oxford, 1913).

COWLEY, A. E. : *The Samaritan Liturgy*, 2 vols. (Oxford, 1909).

GASTER, M. : *The Samaritans*, Schweich Lectures (London, 1923).

—— Article on Samaritans in *Encyclopædia of Islam* (Leyden-London, 1925).

—— " The Samaritan Literature," Supplement to *Encyclopædia of Islam* (1925).

—— *The Asatir : the Samaritan Book of the " Secrets of Moses "* (London, 1927).

GASTER, M. : *The Samaritan Oral Law and Ancient Traditions* (London, 1932).

GEIGER, A. : "Die Gesetzlichen Differenzen zwischen Samaritanern und Juden," *Z.D.M.G.* xx (1866).

HAMMER, H. : *Traktat vom Samaritaner Messias* (Bonn, 1913).

HEIDENHEIM, M. : *Bibliotheca Samaritana*, 3 vols. in one (Leipzig, 1884–96).

KOHN, S. : "Zur Sprache Literatur und Dogmatik der Samaritaner," *Abh. Kunde Morg.*, v. 4 (Leipzig, 1876).

MERX, E. O. A. : "Der Messias oder Ta'eb der Samaritaner," *Beihefte Z.A.W.* 17 (Giessen, 1909).

MONTGOMERY, J. A. : *The Samaritans* (Philadelphia, 1907).

OESTERLEY, W. O. E. : *The Books of the Apocrypha* (London, 1936).

ROTHSTEIN, J. W. : *Juden und Samaritaner* (Leipzig, 1908).

DE SACY, SILVESTRE : *Mémoire sur l'État actuel des Samaritains* (Paris, 1812).

—— "Correspondance des Samaritains de Naplouse," *Notices et Extraits*, xii (1831).

THOMSON, J. E. H. : *The Samaritans* (Edinburgh, 1919).

VILMAR, E. : *Abulfathi Annales Samaritani* (Gotha, 1865).

WRESCHNER, L. : *Samaritanische Traditionen* (Berlin, 1888).

V

THE LAW AND PHARISAISM

BY

R. TRAVERS HERFORD

V

THE LAW AND PHARISAISM [1]

To give an adequate account of Pharisaism, as a connected system of thought and practice, is obviously impossible in a single lecture, and I shall not attempt to do so. The subject is allotted to me as forming part of the more general subject of this course of lectures, which deals with the relation between Law and Religion, as exemplified in some of the principal forms which that relation has assumed in the history of mankind. I shall, accordingly, confine my treatment of Pharisaism within the limits here indicated.

Religion, in some form or another, is found amongst practically all peoples in all ages, and in every stage of development, from the vaguest sense of something or someone divine to the most spiritual worship of the highest religions. And along with, but not always associated with, religion there is always found a feeling of obligation, an influence of some kind which imposes a restraint upon men's actions, so that they are other than what they would have been if there had not been that feeling of obligation, or if it had not been yielded to. There is a something which tends to limit a man's freedom to do just as he likes. It is not a compulsion, but a leading in the direction of doing *this* and away

[1] For a full treatment the reader is referred to the present writer's *The Pharisees* (1924), *Judaism in the New Testament Period* (1928), and *Talmud and Apocrypha* (1933), as well as to G. F. Moore's *Judaism* (1927), especially vol. i, part i, chaps. iii–vi.

from doing *that*. It is the feeling of " ought," and to
call it so is a way of expressing the felt difference
between right and wrong. What the origin of that
feeling may be, or what it really means, has been the
subject of endless philosophical inquiry ; but all the
attempts to explain it necessarily take for granted
that there is something to explain, that this sense of
obligation is a fundamental fact in human nature, at
all events in historic times. Men have always felt so,
and have in various ways acted on their feeling, no
matter how they explained it to themselves, or though
they gave no explanation at all.

I am not concerned with the various explanations
which have been put forth, or the various ways in
which the feeling of obligation has been brought into
connexion with religion. My purpose in this lecture
is to present to you one system of belief and practice
in which the sense of obligation is brought into the
closest possible connexion with religion, so close that
religion and morality (which is based on the sense of
obligation) are inseparably blended and hardly to be
distinguished ; and Law, which ultimately rests on
the sense of obligation, is a part of religion though
not identical with it. This is that particular type of
Judaism to which the name of Pharisaism is given.
It is the development of the religion of Israel along
a line which began with Ezra, continued with the
Sopherim, the early scribes, was taken up by the
Pharisees properly so called, and carried on by
the Rabbis whose teaching and ideas are recorded in
the Talmud and the cognate literature. The line
has continued till the present day. The system so
developed has been consistent throughout in its in-
sistence on certain main principles, whereby it has

acquired the strongly marked character peculiar to itself. Since the fall of Jerusalem in A.D. 70 down to recent times, it has remained, in its essentials, the only important representation of the Jewish religion ; and it would be correct to call it by the name of Pharisaism, if it were not that the name " Pharisee " came into the language at a time later than that at which the movement began, and passed out of common use when the need for a distinguishing name was no longer felt. But, though the name was a temporary label, the principles of the system to which the name was attached remained consistent throughout. With this explanation I may be allowed to use, for convenience, the name Pharisaism to denote the whole system developed along the lines which I have just indicated.

In this sense, Pharisaism begins with Ezra, who was indeed regarded by the Pharisees of later times as their founder and, so to speak, their patron saint. They said of him (b. Sanh. 21ᵇ) that he was worthy to have received the divine revelation from God, if Moses had not already done so. And they expressed their view of his true function by saying (b. Succ. 20ᵃ) that when that divine revelation had been forgotten in Israel, Ezra again founded it, or established it.

Whatever Ezra did, he did not make a complete breach with the past. He had behind him all the religious experience of Israel up till his own time, all the historical development of that religion, all the main ideas and beliefs which served to express it. He had no thought of breaking with these, perhaps no thought of making any innovation in them. What he did was to lay a special stress upon one factor in the religion of Israel as it had been before the Captivity, a factor which had indeed been present in that religion for ages past, but which had been too little regarded or even forgotten. This was the factor of the divine revelation, believed to have been given to Moses on Sinai and by him delivered to the children of Israel. No one ever questioned that that revelation had been made ; but the people who had inherited it had not been faithful in their observance of what was required of them by the terms of that revelation ; and, after repeated warnings by the prophets, the calamity of the Exile was, in the view of Ezra, brought upon them as a punishment for their disobedience and a sharp reminder of their duty.

The divine revelation here referred to was recorded in the five books ascribed to Moses, and known by the name of the Torah, usually but quite wrongly called the Law. Torah never meant Law. It means Teaching, and the five books containing it were accepted as being what God had *taught* concerning His will and His nature. It was this record, as the Torah, or " the Torah of Moses," which Ezra proclaimed and whose authority he established in the Jewish community after his own return from Babylonia. Whether it was the whole Pentateuch which he proclaimed, or only the Priestly Code, does not matter for my present purpose. His proclamation of the Torah was the reminder, to those who heard him, of the divine teaching which had been neglected, the divine will which had been disobeyed, and of the urgent need of a return to the discarded obedience. If the Jews, as a community, were to have a future at all, it could only be achieved by a determined effort on their part to take to heart and put into action the divine teaching ; and to do this not merely as a community but as so many individuals. The sense of obligation to do the will of God, which of course had been present in the Jewish mind for centuries, must now be intensified, so that every separate person could feel it and own its authority over himself. Here was the connexion between religion and the obligation which underlies both morality and law, stressed in the most emphatic manner. Religion was the belief in, and the worship of, God. The only true service of Him was to do His will ; and the authority, which created the obligation so to serve Him, was His authority.

Therefore, when Ezra secured the acceptance of the Torah by the assembled people, he pledged them to take it as the supreme authority for the guidance of their public and private life. He established it in a supremacy which it had never held up till that time. In theory to some extent it had been supreme, but in practice never. But there was a considerable difference between acknowledging a general obligation to do the will of God, and acknowledging the particular obligation to do this and that specific duty set forth in the Torah in a written precept. And Ezra's success in what he set out to do was that he really did persuade a substantial number of the people to own the authority of the Torah in the special and not merely in the general sense. He did not live to see the full accomplishment of his purpose. His view of Torah was disputed in his own time, and for long afterwards ; but it was the Torah, in the supreme position which he asserted for it, which became the ruling factor in the centuries after the fall of Jerusalem.

To have made and maintained such a claim, and to have secured the recognition of it, was to have achieved much ; but Ezra himself knew well that

something more was needed, some continuous pro-
tection for the position he had won. The Torah
which he had established was a body of teaching,
containing precepts and passages of instruction. The
Torah, as the record of a divine revelation, would fail
of its purpose if its contents were not made clear to the
understanding of those to whom the revelation was
given. When Ezra first publicly read the Torah
(Neh. viii. 7–8) there were at his side certain Levites
who " caused the people to understand the Torah . . .
and they read in the book, in the Torah of God,
distinctly ; and they gave the sense, so that they
understood the reading." This had been, indeed,
part of Ezra's plan from the time when he left
Babylonia for Palestine. In Ezra vii. 10 it is stated
that " Ezra had set his heart to ' seek ' the Torah of
the Lord, and to do it, and to teach in Israel statutes
and judgments," where the word translated " seek "
should be rendered " *interpret* " or " *explain*," according
to the regular usage of the later language in reference
to Torah. For Ezra to " seek " the Torah would be
unmeaning. To " interpret " it was of the utmost
importance, not only for his own time but even more
for later times. The Torah contained various precepts,
and to the fulfilment of these precepts every Jew was
individually pledged. He must therefore understand
exactly what it was that he was called upon to do.
He must have it explained to him by someone who
was able to interpret to him the words of the Torah.
Such interpretation was given, perhaps by Ezra
himself, certainly by the teachers who immediately
followed him and who were called the Sopherim, or
Scribes. And the work of interpretation thus begun
has never really ceased from that time to this. It

might be supposed, indeed, that an interpretation
once given by a competent exponent would not need
to be repeated or supplemented. When such a one
had declared, in reference to some precept or passage
in the Torah, " This is what it means," that would
seem to end the matter. If a modern scholar, interpreting a passage in some classic author, declares that
it means so-and-so, he is stating what, in his opinion,
the author really intended to say. But, for the Jewish
interpreter, the object of his labour was to find out
what this or that passage of the Torah meant to the
person who was required to obey it. The difference
would not be felt at first, but, in the succeeding
generations after Ezra, the question addressed to the
interpreter would be, " What has the Torah to say to
me (or to us) now living ? We are not concerned to
know what it may have meant in Ezra's time. We
want to know how exactly it applies to our own
present life." Every Jew, so it was taught in later
times, should regard himself as having been actually
present at Sinai, when the Torah was delivered to
Moses and accepted by all the people. When Ezra
began the practice of interpretation and ensured that
it should be carried on from generation to generation,
he was guarding against the danger that the Torah,
as an ancient sacred book, would come to be looked
upon as merely an antique relic and not as a teacher
able to speak to the needs of each succeeding age.

I may be attributing to Ezra a deeper insight into
the significance of what he did than he really
possessed ; but what I have said does, I believe,
correctly indicate what the interpretation of Torah
really did aim at and has continued to aim at ; and
it serves to show why all the written material of the

H

Talmud and Midrash is in the form of interpretation
of Torah. Those whose words and names are
recorded in that literature were not theologians
framing a system of doctrine, or philosophers defining
a body of thought, or professional moralists laying
down a theory of ethics ; they were teachers who tried
to show to their fellow men and women what the
divine revelation recorded in the Torah meant to
them, what their duty was and how they could rightly
fulfil it. The object of these teachers was intensely
practical ; it was a discipline, not a mere course of
instruction, and by the method of interpretation they
were able to bring the authority of the Torah to bear
upon every individual conscience of those whom they
could influence, in each succeeding age.

The Sopherim, then, made it their business to
interpret the Torah, to explain exactly what it
intended to teach to those who had accepted it. The
written word of the text needed to be amplified where
it was not sufficiently precise, to be more closely
defined where its statements were only in general
terms, to be brought to bear upon questions which
were not dealt with in the original, and so on.
Accordingly the oldest form which the Sopherim gave
to their interpretation was that of a sort of verse-by-
verse commentary on the written text of the Torah,
a process known as Midrash. This method was never
wholly abandoned, although a new method was
introduced by the successors of the Sopherim, as I
shall explain presently.

The results obtained from the interpretation of
Torah by the Sopherim were of two kinds, because
the subject-matter with which they dealt was twofold
in its contents. Part of the Torah was preceptive,

consisting of precise commands—Thou shalt, or Thou shalt not. All the rest was non-preceptive. Accordingly—and this is the point of connexion between Torah and Law—interpretation of the preceptive part aimed at giving a clear direction how the precept in question ought to be obeyed. God had commanded Israel to do so-and-so. There must be some one exactly right way of carrying out His command, and that exactly right way, if it were not known or not certain, must be sought until it was found. It was the work of the interpreters to find it, and to state it, when found, in precise terms. Such a statement was called a " *halachah*," and it served the purpose of a rule of right conduct. The word means " walking," from *halach*, to go. And, as a rule of right conduct, it was a direction indicating to a man how in a given case he should *walk* in the ways of the Lord.

The interpretation of the non-preceptive part of the Torah had for its result no such definite statement— nothing at all events that could be regarded as a rule binding on those who received it. Its intention was to set forth what was implied in the teaching of the Torah about God, His nature and His ways, His dealings with man, and man's relation to Him. And the result so obtained was called " *haggadah*," which means " declaration," and signifies that the Torah declares so-and-so. Haggadah, therefore, is the interpretation of the Torah on its non-preceptive side. And this is the true meaning of Haggadah ; it does not mean fanciful narrative, legend, or the like, although it often took those forms. The only qualification which should be added is that the Haggadah was extended so as to take in all the rest of Scripture, and not the Torah alone, as its subject-matter.

It is probable that of the words halachah and haggadah, haggadah is the older. At the beginning, when the object in view was to interpret the Torah as a whole, it was sufficient to say that the Torah " declared," " *higgid*," so-and-so, and the result was called haggadah. But later, when it was found necessary to distinguish between the preceptive and the non-preceptive parts of the Torah, the word " halachah " was introduced to indicate the results of interpretation as it affected conduct, and the word haggadah was restricted so as to cover only the non-preceptive parts of the Torah. However, and whenever, these two famous words came into use—and they cannot have been later than the period of the Sopherim—they have remained ever since as technical terms of the interpretation of the Torah, in the respective meanings which I have assigned to them.

The period of the Sopherim came to an end about the year 270 B.C. Their organization as a teaching body, such as it was, ceased to function ; and for nearly a century there was no authority to take its place. There was, that is, no body of persons competent to define the halachah in any given case. This " decline and fall " of the Sopherim is almost certainly connected with the change from Persian to Greek rule, and more particularly with the fact that Judea came under the rule of either an Egyptian or a Syrian king, and was brought, for good perhaps but certainly for evil, under the influence of Hellenism. And one consequence of that change in the political condition of the Jews was that new ideas and practices were introduced or allowed to grow up, in regard to which there was no one to say whether, or how, they were related to the Torah ; no one competent to discover and define a halachah concerning them. Yet, if this could not be done, there was danger lest the Jewish religion, as developed by the Sopherim on the lines already indicated, would, so to speak, get out of hand and gradually lose all connexion with the Torah, and the Torah itself would cease to be the guide of life, and become merely an antique relic, a monument of ancient piety, whose claim to obedience was no longer recognized or acted upon.

From the point of view of those who followed the line of the Sopherim in regard to the Torah, this was a serious and pressing danger ; and the means by which they met and disarmed it marks a most important change in the development of Pharisaism. In form, it was hardly more than a change in the method of interpretation of the Torah ; in substance, it was a change in the essential meaning of the Torah itself, and it made possible the future development of Judaism, one might say, without limit. This new feature was the concept of the *Unwritten Torah*, a concept whose implications were hardly recognized at first, but which proved to be of far-reaching importance for all the succeeding history of Judaism. Let me try to explain what the change was and what was involved in it.

The halachah was the direction that a certain precept was to be performed in a certain manner ; and it was deduced by interpreting the written word of the Torah, or it was in some way connected with the text. If it had not been, it could have no claim to be received and obeyed. The Torah had been solemnly accepted, and the people pledged to obey it. Whatever was offered to them by the religious teachers must be included in the meaning of the Torah, must

be a part of the Torah, shown in greater detail by the
process of competent interpretation. And this process
had been sufficient during the time of the Sopherim.
But when, in the period after them, the new ideas
and practices came in, of which I have spoken, either
these must be rejected and forbidden, or else they
must in some way be brought within the range of the
authority of the Torah. Some of these new ideas and
practices which had gradually come in were evidently
good and such as ought to be recognized, but there
was no support for them in the written Torah. They
were not expressly mentioned in the text, and there
was no method of interpretation which would establish the required connexion.

The idea occurred to someone amongst the teachers
of Torah, that there must be a tradition behind these
ideas and practices (though they seemed to lie outside
the Torah), a tradition which would account for their
being held and practised. If that were so, then it
would follow that the divine revelation was not
confined to the written text of the Torah. There must
be an unwritten Torah, not as the rival or even the
commentary on the text, but as completing it ; so
that the written and unwritten together made up *the*
Torah as it essentially was. This new idea appeared
and began to be acted on somewhere about the year
170 B.C., and was only accepted with much hesitation,
and at first by only a few of the teachers. For, of
course, the new idea rested on a pure assumption,
viz. that there was a tradition, going back, as it must
have done, to the time of Moses. And the teachers
of Torah, whom we may now call the Pharisees, were
quite aware of the weakness of their case in respect
to its foundation. But they maintained it nevertheless,

and justified their action in doing so by the results which they obtained from this new conception of Torah.

The immediate result was that it became possible to define a halachah without basing it on some text of the written Torah, or even establishing any connexion with the text. The halachah, so defined, was vouched for by a tradition, assumed to have come down from the far-off past, and accepted on the authority of the teachers who declared it. And, by means of this concept of the Unwritten Torah, these teachers were enabled to give a wider meaning to the precepts of the written Torah, being no longer tied down to the literal sense or the interpretation of it on the former lines. For the Torah was now understood to be the whole revelation, contained in the written text and the unwritten tradition taken together. And that revelation was taken to be the whole not only of what at any time was understood to be its meaning, *but of what might hereafter at any time be shown to be implied in it.* Torah was held to be the divine revelation, immeasurable and inexhaustible ; and Torah, at any one time, was so much of that revelation as had come within the understanding of those to whom it had been given. All had been imparted to Moses, so it was held ; and whatever might be, at any future time, unfolded as its meaning by some acute and far-seeing teacher, was contained in the Torah as Moses had received it. This conception of Torah was certainly held in the period of the Talmudic teachers, and it explains the meaning of the change made by those successors of the Sopherim who first introduced the Unwritten Torah. But I think it probable that they had at first no clear perception of what they were really doing, or of the fuller meaning of Torah which was dawning on their minds. Be this as it may, the new method of defining the halachah, without connecting it with Scripture, gave them a liberty of interpretation which they had never had before. It enabled them to modify, or even to set aside, the written word in order to bring out its real intention, or rather the real intention of God who had caused the sacred text to be written, but who had not confined His whole meaning to what was written therein. The way was thus opened for an advance from the literal meaning of the text towards a higher, and especially an *ethically* higher, meaning, one more in accordance with the rising moral standard of the times since the text was written. Two instances will show how this was done.

One is the famous text of the *lex talionis*,[1] " an eye for an eye and a tooth for a tooth," etc. There is a clearly stated order that in certain cases of bodily injury a savage retaliation was to be inflicted. Those who defined the halachah dealing with such cases frankly abolished the written text, and made no attempt to humanize it by any artifice of interpretation. They appointed a different procedure to be followed in such cases, viz. the payment of a money fine, depending on the amount of the injury. And, in the passage in the Mishnah (M. B. *Kamma*, viii. 1) where such cases are dealt with, and in the discussion of the passage in the Gemara, there is no hint that the old savage law had ever been enforced and had later been changed. There is rather the opinion that no one could ever have been so cruel and brutal as to

[1] [See Murphy, *above*, p. 18 f., and editor's notes ; also Loewe, vol. i, p. 146 f.—ED.]

take the written command literally. The written command became obsolete at a very early time : perhaps indeed it was never acted on. It is therefore grossly unfair to say that the principle of " an eye for an eye and a tooth for a tooth " is a principle of the Jewish religion. If it ever were so—and there is nothing to show that it was ever acted on—this had ceased to be true before Christianity had appeared. Jews are no more liable to the charge than Christians are. It is by no means true that the Jewish religion can be understood by taking the written words of the Torah, or of the Old Testament as a whole, in their literal meaning.

Here is another case in which a direct command contained in the written text, not merely of the Torah but even of the Decalogue, was deliberately set aside. The Decalogue said : " Thou shalt observe the Sabbath day. . . . In it thou shalt do no manner of work," etc.—a command as definite and precise as words could make it. Yet this was, in certain cases, entirely disregarded and even flatly disobeyed. Those cases were such as involved danger to life. If a human life was endangered by illness or injury, then any and every law implied in the observance of the Sabbath not only *might* be but *must* be broken in order to save life. The persons in attendance on the sick or injured man were bound to do, regardless of the Sabbath, whatever was necessary to save his life, without stopping to ask permission from anyone (see *b. Joma*, 84[b]). The Sabbath, no doubt, was a divinely appointed institution, and, as such, to be reverently observed. But a human life was more than an institution, inasmuch as a man, every man, was made in the image and likeness of God. The great truth

that " the Sabbath was made for man and not man
for the Sabbath " was understood by the Rabbis quite
independently of Jesus, and formulated by them in
almost the same words.[1]   They had come to recognize
and act on the principle long before the time of Jesus.
Probably it goes back to the time soon after the
Maccabean Revolt.

These are not the only cases in which the written
text of the Torah was deliberately set on one side or
even flatly disobeyed.   And the halachah which was
defined in such cases was only made possible by the
introduction of the concept of the Unwritten Torah,
whereby the connexion was cut between the halachah
and the written text.

It might seem that by the use of this concept of the
Unwritten Torah there would no longer be any place
for, or any need of, the written Torah.   But this was
not the case ; and those who defined the halachah on
the lines of the Unwritten Torah never understood it
in that way.   Thus, they never dreamed of abolishing
the Sabbath, because it was expressly commanded in
the Torah that it should be observed.   They only said
that in certain cases it must give way to a yet higher
consideration, viz. the sacredness of human life.   In
every other case the obligation remained to observe
the Sabbath.   So, too, the Torah expressly sanctioned,
or even commanded, divorce.   Those who defined the
halachah on the subject by no means wholly approved
of divorce, or rather they were quite aware of the evils
and abuses attendant on unrestricted liberty of divorce.
What they did, and all that they could do, was to

---

[1] [See the present writer's *Talmud and Apocrypha*, p. 115 ff., for
a full statement ; also Loewe, vol. i, pp. 165–177, with special
reference to Jesus' attitude.—ED.]

restrain that liberty, to make the way of divorce difficult, to secure so far as possible the rights of the divorced wife, and to discourage the reckless practice of divorce. They could not, and certainly did not, declare that divorce was in itself wrong and never under any circumstances to be allowed. Only if they had declared that, would they or could they have abolished the express teaching of the Torah on the subject ; and, if they had done that, they would have virtually repudiated the Torah altogether.[1]

These instances which I have given—and many others might be added [2]—show that the application of the concept of the Unwritten Torah made possible the development of the halachah in an ethical direction and not towards a mere elaboration of ritual and ceremony. Of course the halachah had for its object the performance of certain acts ; but these were for the most part such as would serve to express a higher moral purpose, would conform to a higher moral standard, than that of the older times. For the moral standard *did* rise in the course of the centuries of Israel's history, as indeed is evident to any intelligent reader of the Old Testament. And the Pharisees were quite aware of the fact, while at the same time they looked on the Scriptures in general and the Torah in particular as the record of what God had revealed. What they did was to lay stress on the ethically higher elements in Scripture and to leave the lower ones alone, or, where they were obliged to notice those

[1] [See also *Talmud and Apocrypha*, p. 122 f.—ED.]

[2] [E.g. Hillel's institution of *Prosbol*, see *loc. cit.*, p. 119, and Loewe, vol. i, p. 144. Consult *Talmud and Apocrypha*, Book ii, chap. vi, for a lucid treatment of the basic principles of the formation of the Halachah, and the editor's summary, *below*, pp. 173 ff. —ED.]

lower elements, to explain them away by various
far-fetched and fantastic devices, while maintaining at
the same time the higher ethical standard which in
their own reason and conscience they had come to
recognize.

Indeed, one may say with truth that the whole
purpose of elaborating the halachah, at all events after
the concept of the Unwritten Torah had been introduced, was to bring the Torah into accordance with
the higher moral standard, as it was discerned and
recognized by the teachers who defined the halachah
in each generation. If it had been thought sufficient
to do the things commanded in the Torah in their
bare literal meaning, there would have been no need
of any halachah, but there would have been a growing
divergence between the Torah and the consciences of
those who were pledged to obey it. The halachah
was the means of adjustment, by which that divergence
was avoided and the Torah enabled to keep its place
as the supreme authority in each succeeding age, the
continuous revelation of the living God, speaking to
His people in the actual present and not merely in the
far past. The conception of the Unwritten Torah, and
the halachah developed in accordance with it, re-
covered, for Judaism in general and for Pharisaism
in particular, the reality of a living religion for all
purposes. And nothing is further from the truth than
to say that Pharisaism made the Jewish religion, the
religion of the prophets, into a hard and barren
formalism with no spiritual value in it. The truth
rather is that the Pharisees took up the religion of
the prophets and brought it to bear upon the lives
of the people in a way and to an extent which the
prophets had never been able to accomplish. And,

paradoxical though it may sound, it is not far from
the truth to say that if it had not been for the Pharisees
and what they did, the prophets would never have
been heard of. Be this as it may, the Pharisees
certainly developed their ideas of the Unwritten
Torah and the halachah based on it with a clear and
conscious reference to the teaching of the prophets.

The Pharisaic teachers were diligent students of the
writings of the prophets ; indeed it was due to those
teachers that the prophetical books were collected and
arranged in approximately their present form, so that
they could be regarded as the second main division of
the Scriptures, the first being, of course, the Torah.
The prophetical writings were carefully read and
their teaching taken to heart by those who at the same
time were defining halachah with the help of the
Unwritten Torah. One result of such study was to
raise the moral standard for those who meditated on
their words, and this was one main reason why the
halachah was felt to be necessary and made to serve
as a means of adjusting the precepts of the Torah to
the more enlightened moral sense of each succeeding
age. In this way the halachah represented the
application of the prophetic ideas to the Torah. The
prophets had been teachers of righteousness, whatever
else they were. The Pharisaic teachers had precisely
the same object in view, and sought and found most
valuable help towards attaining that object in the
close study of the prophets. But the teaching of the
prophets had, to all appearance, been disregarded by
those to whom it had been addressed, and all their
rebukes and warnings had been powerless to prevent
the disaster of the Exile. This gives the clue to the
work of Ezra and all his successors. A new means

must be found for driving home the lesson of obedience
to the divine will, as taught alike in the Torah and
by the prophets ; and the means which was devised
and set to work was the halachah. And that is why
the whole system of Pharisaism was a discipline and
not merely a body of teaching. Those who came
under the Pharisaic discipline were not allowed to get
off with merely knowing what the divine will was :
they were required to *do* it, and to do it in a carefully
defined way. In thus establishing a discipline, the
Pharisees held, and truly held, that they were carrying
out the work of the prophets, and moreover doing
what the prophets had never been able to do, viz.
secure the actual obedience of the people to the divine
will. They claimed to be the rightful successors of
the prophets, and they expressed that by saying
" Prophecy was taken from the prophets and given
to the Wise [i.e. the Pharisaic teachers], and from
these it has not been taken away " (*b. B. Bathra*, 12ª).
In that acute saying more is implied than might at
first appear. The halachah, as I have said, was the
application of the ideas of the prophets to the interpretation of the Torah ; and the halachah, developed by the help of the concept of the Unwritten
Torah, represented the recognition, in the minds of
the Pharisaic teachers, of a higher ethical standard.
In other words, they interpreted the Torah by the
light of their own reason and conscience, and defined
the halachah accordingly. The prophets had not
defined halachah, certainly ; but they spoke out of
their own reason and conscience, and out of that
intense conviction were able to declare " Thus saith
the Lord." The Pharisaic teachers did not use that
form of speech. They did not need to do so, for they

had the warrant of the Torah, as the express revelation of God, for all that they said. But, no less than the prophets, they felt that they had "the words of the living God"; and the halachah which they defined was a far more effective means than the prophets had ever found of making the divine word attended to and obeyed. To set the Pharisees in any sort of opposition to the prophets is entirely unwarranted. Pharisaism is Applied Prophecy, and the halachah, in the manner of its formation, and in the terms of Torah, represents the prophetic "freedom of speech."

I said at the outset that it was impossible to give an adequate account of Pharisaism within the compass of a single lecture. And even what I have said hitherto would not be sufficient if the real purpose of this lecture is to be fulfilled. I said that the interpretation of Torah took the two forms of halachah and haggadah, according as it dealt with the preceptive and the non-preceptive portions respectively. I have had to confine myself entirely to the growth and meaning of the halachah, and I shall not, even now, be able to spare any time to the haggadah. Yet both these are essential elements in Pharisaism, and must be given due weight in any attempt to estimate the importance of that system. And the reason why Judaism has been called a merely legal religion, and why the word Torah has persistently been rendered by Nomos or Law, is that those who have so misjudged have taken account only of the halachah, which is in a sense Law, and have left out the haggadah, probably because they knew nothing about it. The halachah, which gave directions to perform certain actions, came under the notice of non-Jewish observers, at all events in its results; such observers could see that the Jew

did certain things, sometimes in themselves trivial, as
a religious duty ; but they could not see beyond the
outward act, they could not read the inward intention
with which those acts were done, nor did they usually
stay to ask whether there was an inward intention
which would explain and justify those acts. It is out
of such superficial observations that the charge of
hypocrisy has been constantly brought against the
Pharisees, a charge to which indeed the peculiar form
of halachah is especially liable, but which is none the
more justified on that account. I merely note this in
passing, because I do not want to digress into controversial topics. My purpose throughout has been to
explain as well as I can what I may call the theory of
Pharisaism, the main ideas on which it was based, and
by the development of which it came to be what it
was. I shall devote the remainder of this lecture to the
discussion of certain questions which must arise in any
proper study of Pharisaism, and which are in strict
accordance with the governing purpose of the whole
of this series of lectures. These questions are : What
is the real obligation of which the halachah is the
expression ?   What is the relation of conscience to
the Torah ?   In what sense and to what extent is
Pharisaism a religion of law ? These are, indeed, not
so much separate questions as various aspects of one
question, viz. : How is the sense of obligation, inherent
in human nature, accounted for and made effective
in Pharisaism ? What I have already said about
halachah will help to provide the answer.

The entire *corpus* of the halachah, as it was gradually
elaborated, codified in the Mishnah and finally
embodied in the Talmud, was intended to cover the
whole, and did actually cover the greater part, of the

actions and relations of life, or as much as could be included of those which would commonly form part of the life of the Jew. The halachah was binding on every member of the community, on those at least who accepted the system. No one was bound to accept it, and no one was punished for not accepting it. Of those who did accept it, only such as did not conform to it were punished, and *that* by being subject to disapproval more or less strongly expressed. I am not concerned at present with those who did not come under the system. For those who did, the halachah was, in the strict sense of the word, Law. The halachah was Law, the Torah was not Law. As law, the halachah covered the ground of both civil and criminal law, and the whole *corpus* of halachah was, in form at all events, a legal code.

So also, looked at from another point of view, the halachah covered the field of morality, dealing with right and wrong actions, and the obligation of con-science—in short, with the moral law in general. On the legal side and on the moral side, the halachah imposed, and was framed for the purpose of imposing, a considerable amount of restraint upon a man's freedom of action. But it is important to notice that neither on the legal nor on the moral side are the abstract terms used which are commonly found in legal or ethical treatises. There are no words for either " law " or " equity," though the meaning of both was well understood. There is no word for " conscience," nor for the " moral law," nor even for " religion," though again the meaning of these was perfectly familiar. Such abstract terms only became necessary when the leaders of Jewish thought began to write philosophical treatises ; and they did not do so till long after the Talmud was closed. Those with whom I am concerned, the teachers who defined and developed the halachah, never wrote books at all, philosophical or any other. And, what is more important, they were not engaged in working out a *theory*, of ethics or of anything else. They were not in any technical sense moralists or philosophers or theologians or jurists. Teachers they certainly were ; but their " colleges " or " academies " or " schools," sometimes spoken of in books on Jewish subjects written usually by non-Jewish authors, were not colleges or academies in the usual sense of the words. They were places where the teachers of Torah could gather their disciples and impress on them what the Torah was, what it meant, and what it required, all in as minute detail as they could. From first to last, from Ezra to the men who closed the Talmud about a thousand years after his time, the one and only object of the Pharisaic teachers was to interpret the Torah, and to teach it not as a body of thought, a system of doctrine, but as a guide to action, viz. the practical service of God by the doing of right actions and the refraining from wrong ones. They had no need to start from first principles and begin by in-quiring into the basis of the moral law in human nature, the nature of conscience, and so on, and then connecting these up with the Torah. They began with the Torah, and needed nothing more. There they had, as they held with unquestioning conviction, the full and inexhaustible revelation of the divine will. There they were told what they should do, and they studied to learn, with more and more exact detail, how they should do it. And there they had the one and only reason for doing it, viz. that God commanded them to do it. That was the obligation, and the authority which created the obligation was His authority.

Of course the Pharisaic teachers did not invent this statement of their task, or this view of the ethical aspect of human nature. They inherited all the religious and moral experience of the ages before their time, as recorded in the Scriptures. They inherited the belief that man was a free moral agent, whose service must be a voluntary choice if it were to have any moral worth. They knew of no other sanction than the will of God, as revealed in the Torah, for right action. And they could only discern what was revealed in the Torah, as the will of God, by the light of their own reason and conscience. The whole of their ideas of religion and morality were based on the recorded and inherited experience of their predecessors in Old Testament times. And the only innovation which they made was to elevate the Torah into a position of especial eminence, and to lay all the emphasis in their power upon practical obedience to its precepts. So they were not concerned with the theoretical side of morality, nor with morality as a separate subject of study, nor even with religion as a separate subject of study. Religion and morality were inseparably blended in the conception of a conscious relation to God which involved the devotion of their whole mental activity to Him, in thought, belief and worship, and the obeying of His commandments in the practical conduct of life. And thus it is that, for the Pharisees, the whole of their spiritual life was conditioned by, and realized in, the conception of Torah, the full and inexhaustible revelation which God had given.

The contrast between Pharisaic Judaism and other forms of religion, notably Christianity, is usually expressed by saying that the Jew is under the constraint of an external law, while the adherents of other forms of religion are free to act according to their consciences. Whatever truth there may be in this contrast, it is certainly not the whole truth. And I will devote the remainder of this lecture to the question, What was the position of the Pharisee in regard to freedom of choice in his actions ? Was he bound by an external law, or was he free ?

That he was under an obligation to do right and to refrain from wrong goes without saying. It is so in every moral system. The obligation is the feeling of " ought," and without that there could be no morality. The obligation is a form of restraint or constraint. He who feels it owns in it a certain authority having a rightful claim to his obedience. It is not an authority which he himself has set up, or could have set up. It is in that sense an external authority. But, as he owns it in his own mind, it is an internal authority. Obviously he could not own it otherwise than in his own mind. Further, the obligation is not a compulsion. It does not force him to do the act which it points out, it merely indicates that he ought to do it, and leaves him free to choose whether or not he will do it. This is so in whatever form the sense of " ought " is recognized. It would be so if the obligation were conceived as a command, i.e. a definite law, because the subject of a command is in the last resort free to choose whether he will obey it or not. A command does not become a forcible compulsion until violence is used, and then the action ceases to be moral at all.

Now the whole of the Pharisaic conception of moral action is based on the obligation to do the will of God. The obligation comes to him in the form of a command—Thou shalt, or Thou shalt not. Its authority is the authority of God, who alone has the right to command. It is made known to him in the Torah ; but, unless he had a mind and a conscience, he could never receive the revelation, or feel the obligation of the commands contained in it. It is not the Torah, or even the halachah, to which his obedience is due, or for which it is rightfully claimed. This is due to God alone, who gave the Torah as the means of *teaching* to Israel what he ought to do. To do the will of God is the end and aim of the Pharisaic discipline. The Torah teaches him what that will is, and the halachah shows it to him in greater and greater detail. But Torah, and more particularly halachah, are only directions given to him *how to do* what is commanded, that will of God which it is his duty to do. In everything which he does, in obedience to the obligation which he owns, he is serving God by doing His will. Every occasion for doing so is an opportunity for service of God. And, unless he did the act commanded with the conscious purpose of serving, his act—according to the Pharisees—would have no worth, moral or religious. The theory of the *opus operatum* was definitely ruled out by the Pharisaic teachers.

Every act which the Jew owned to be a duty he represented to himself as a thing commanded, and he called it a Mitzvah. And accordingly, every mitzvah was an opportunity offered to him of serving God. It might be a precept of but small range and trivial importance, and it might be anything up to the

supreme and all-inclusive mitzvah "Thou shalt love
the Lord thy God." Whatever it was, apparently
great or small, it was what God willed that he should
do. The Pharisee delighted in the abundance of the
mitzvoth, and regarded them as signs of God's beneficence to His people. This is the reverse side of what
is known in other connexions as the " burden of the
Law." What the Jew felt about it, and still in large
measure feels, is expressed in the term " *simḥah shel
mitzvah*," " the joy of the commandment "—a term
which would never have been used if the commandment had been felt as a burden.[1]

The Jew, in all this, was and remained a free moral
agent. If he had not been, neither Torah nor halachah
nor mitzvah would have had any meaning for him,
or any authority over him. But what if his conscience
bid him do some act which the halachah told him not
to do ? What then ? Was he in that case free to go
against the halachah ? That is a question which
would naturally suggest itself to those who are not, so
to speak, under the halachah. And the urgency of it
would only be felt by those who, for whatever reason,
doubted the validity of the halachah as a system and
the wisdom of the teachers who worked it out. Within
the system—i.e. assuming the validity of the halachah
and the wisdom of the teachers—the question could
hardly arise, and, so far as I have read in the Talmudic
literature, it never did arise. If a Jew were confronted
with an occasion for doing something, and if he had
in the Torah the divine command to do it, and in the
halachah the particular direction *how* to do it, a
direction given by teachers whom he trusted and who
were, moreover, the accepted leaders of the whole

[1] [See on this term also Loewe, vol. i, pp. 138 ff.—Ed.]

community, then there would be nothing for conscience to urge in the opposite direction. So long as Torah, halachah and mitzvah were to him the means by which he was taught the divine will, his conscience would naturally urge him in the same direction, and he would do the act, whatever it was, with thankfulness to God for giving him the opportunity of service, and to the teachers who had shown him how he should perform that mitzvah, and so obey the divine will.

The word mitzvah is indeed one of the key-words of Pharisaism. It represents what, in other systems of ethics, is expressed by the word " ought," the fundamental sense of obligation. It is applied to every act which a man feels that he ought to do, and by the doing of which he serves God, and he does it as the fulfilment of a divine command. The halachah is not co-extensive with mitzvah ; for the halachah was only possible when the particular mitzvah could be defined, as in the case of negative precepts, and such positive precepts as were necessarily restricted in their range. But it was a mitzvah to show kindness, brotherly love, sympathy, pity, and so on. These were not definable in any halachah, and the attempt so to define them was never made. Instead, these were said to be " committed to the heart," meaning that they were left to the inspiration of the kind heart and the generous feeling at the moment when they were called for. And the first and great commandment, " Thou shalt love the Lord thy God," and the second, which is like unto it, " Thou shalt love thy neighbour as thyself," included everything, great or small, which could be thought of as mitzvah, but they were never defined in a halachah. Which means that while the halachah prescribed the mode of action of a man at this point and at that, the mitzvah covered the whole of his life. At no point was he outside the range of the obligation to do the divine will. In everything he did, in all his waking hours, there was the opportunity to serve God.

He asked for no reason why he should do this except that it was the divine will. He did not do it for the sake of any reward. There is indeed frequent mention of reward and merit in the literature of Pharisaism, and those terms had a definite meaning ; but they were never to be the *motives* for doing the will of God. The Torah was to be obeyed always for its own sake, *lishmah*, and for no lower reason than that. " The reward of a mitzvah is a mitzvah," said Ben Azai. A man who serves God in the doing of a mitzvah could hope for nothing better than to be given the opportunity to perform another. And the highest type of service is that of the man who serves God for love. Paul was not the only one to teach that love is the fulfilling of the Law.

The sketch of Pharisaism which I have set before you is incomplete because it does not include the vast range of the haggadah. Also, I have not attempted to indicate the history of the Pharisees, except in its earliest period. I have tried to show you what may be called the theory of Pharisaism, the main ideas and principles on which their whole system was based. That the account I have given differs widely from the usual conceptions of Pharisaism I am well aware. I have given it as the result of my own rather long study of the Talmudic literature. And what I have been most concerned to show is that the object in view of the Pharisaic teachers was to set up a discipline, not to teach a doctrine, let alone a whole theology.

They sought to intensify the natural feeling of obligation, and to do so, not in order to bring it into connexion with religion, but because it was already there,
and only needed to be more clearly discerned and
more faithfully obeyed. The Torah was given to them
for this purpose, and they fulfilled that purpose with
a zeal and perseverance which were not exhausted
after a thousand years. They were only human : they
made mistakes, and perhaps failed to see some things
which others have seen. But what they did is surely
one of the greatest attempts ever made in history to
bring the actions of men into close relation with their
sense of duty and their belief in God. Torah, mitzvah
and halachah were the means by which they sought
to effect this, and the practical discipline was the
scene of action. For the Pharisee, Law and Religion
were inseparably blended—Law, not in the sense of a
statute or a code, but in the sense of the recognition
of the supreme authority of God, and Religion as the
response of man to that feeling of authority. The
Torah was the revelation to the Pharisee of what all
these great assertions meant ; and to him its highest
word was, and necessarily was, "*Thou shalt* love the
Lord thy God with all thy heart and with all thy soul
and with all thy mind."

VI
JESUS, PAUL, AND THE LAW

BY

T. W. MANSON

VI

JESUS, PAUL, AND THE LAW [1]

MORE than thirty years ago Wrede dealt with this very question in his little book on Paul. He argued that while Jesus and Paul both laid violent hands on the Law, they did so from very different motives. He puts the matter thus :

> " Jesus' attack on the character of the Law is always of a moral kind. He assails the institutions when and because they slay the moral sense, rob the soul of piety, substitute appearance for reality. Where in Paul's work do we find such an ethical criticism of legalism ? He

---

[1] In this article I have attempted to do two things :

(a) I have tried to state as clearly as I could what I take to be the essential points in the attitude of Jesus and Paul to the Law. There are statements in the Gospels and in the Pauline Epistles which may seem to be incompatible with the positions laid down in this paper. It would take far more space than is available to deal with these. Some of the Gospel matter I should regard as unauthentic ; and, in the case of Paul, I think it must be admitted that his natural pride in his Jewish birth prevented him from always carrying his doctrine to its rigorous conclusion.

(b) I have not attempted either to justify or to correct what I find in the New Testament. Such as it is, the statement is as objective as I can make it. Much that is in it may seem harsh to devout Jews ; but the issue that was joined in the New Testament was a real issue and the Church and the Synagogue did fall out over it. I am only concerned to show why they fell out.

[The reader is referred to L. Baeck's " Judaism in the Church " in *Hebrew Union College Annual*, ii (1925), for a Jewish view of the problem.—ED.]

fights against the Law as a missionary, and as the advocate of redemption in Christ. That is another matter." [1]

The kind of revolution that has taken place in one generation may be seen by taking this statement of Emil Brunner's :

" The key to the ethics of the New Testament is contained in the following passages : *Romans vi, vii*, and the beginning of *Romans viii*. Here, as nowhere else, we perceive in great clearness and detail the identity of the central points in dogmatics and in ethics. The Sermon on the Mount, on the other hand, although it is the necessary presupposition of Christian ethics, is not its foundation. Its relation to *Romans vi* is that of the Law to the Gospel." [2]

Wrede saw the issue between Jesus and the Law crystallized in the simple precepts of the Sermon on the Mount over against the elaborate casuistry of the Scribes : he saw the opposition of Paul to the Law as a conflict between Gospel and Law. It is the former interpretation that is now challenged : and for a variety of reasons.

(1) It is realized that the simplicity of the Sermon on the Mount does not mean that its demands are thereby easier of fulfilment than those of the Law. On the contrary, if with St. Peter (Acts xv. 10) we describe the Law as " a yoke which neither our fathers nor we were able to bear," we should have to regard the " New Law " of the Sermon on the Mount as a still more intolerable and impossible burden. Whatever Jesus may have meant when He said " My yoke is easy, and my burden is light," He can hardly have had in mind the extremely searching and exacting demands of the sermon.

---

[1] *Paul*, p. 160.   [2] *The Divine Imperative*, p. 586.

(2) It is more and more coming to be realized that what Jesus offered to men was not good advice or even a good example, but good news—the announcement of the Kingdom of God as a present and beneficent reality. As such it comes primarily saying not " Thou shalt " and " Thou shalt not," but " Ask and you shall receive ; seek and you shall find ; knock and it shall be opened to you " ; or " All things are ready : come to the marriage feast." The business of Jesus as conceived by Jesus is not to intensify the pressure of the obligations of the Law, but rather to bring a renewal of spiritual health and vigour to those who could make no sort of headway with the existing demands. " They that are whole have no need of the physician, but they that are sick." It is most necessary to realize at the outset that the task which Jesus took in hand was not the reform of the Torah but the re-creation of men and women who could not obey the Torah, much less the Sermon on the Mount.

From the beginning Christianity means New Life rather than New Rules of Life. That is, from the beginning it is a message of salvation, the announcement that the power of God is abroad in the world for the uplifting of the fallen and the ingathering of the rejected and despised. On this issue there is fundamental agreement between the preaching of Jesus and the letters of Paul.

(3) The background of the Ministry of Jesus and the apostolic campaigns of Paul is fundamentally the same. This fact has been obscured by a wrong and one-sided emphasis on the ethical teaching of Jesus and on the doctrine of Justification *sola fide* in Paul. There *is* ethical teaching in the teaching of Jesus, and Justification *sola fide* is certainly part of Paul's

exposition of Christianity. But the Ministry of Jesus
is far more than ethical precepts, and the Gospel
preached by Paul is far more than Justification by
faith as against justification ἐξ ἔργων νόμου.

The essential thing for the understanding both of
the Ministry of Jesus and the theology of Paul is the
doctrine of the two kingdoms : the Kingdom of God
and the kingdom of Satan. All the evils under which
men suffer, and all the evils which they commit, may
be regarded as the manifestation in history of the
power of the evil kingdom. All men's hopes for the
future—the future of the world or of the individual—
are bound up with the triumph of the Kingdom of
God over the kingdom of Satan. That, when it comes,
is the coming of the Kingdom of God in power. That
is the theme of the apocalypses : it is represented as
the hope of many in Israel in the songs which are
introduced into the first two chapters of St. Luke's
Gospel. It is not, perhaps, going too far to say that
at the beginning of the Christian era there was
scarcely a devout soul in Israel that was not looking
for the coming of the kingdom, though there were
certainly differences in the way in which the coming
kingdom was imagined.

That is the essential point : the movement which
originates with Jesus and is carried on by Paul is at
bottom eschatological, and only secondarily is it concerned with the matters which were the business of
the Scribes.

The difference between Jewish apocalyptic on the
one hand and Jesus and Paul on the other is that both
Jesus and Paul have exchanged the future—even the
futurum instans—for the present tense. For Jesus and
Paul the Kingdom of God has in some real sense come.

Not only so : it has come in an unexpected way. Right up to the preaching of John the Baptist the coming kingdom is proclaimed as a coming judgment : a sifting of men and nations and a ruthless condemnation and destruction of all that is evil, all that is contrary to the Law. But as proclaimed by Jesus the kingdom has come as a manifestation of divine grace and mercy. It is an invitation to sinners. It is God giving with both hands to the unthankful and evil. Jesus casting out demons, healing the sick, befriending the publican and harlot, is—that is the message of the Gospels—the Kingdom of God in action. What we call the Ministry (lit. *service*) of Jesus *is* the Rule of God.

What is the bearing of all this on the Law ? It is very simple and, I think, vitally important. For Jesus the thing of first importance, the only thing of *any* importance, is His own Ministry, that is to say, His task of manifesting the perfect rule of God by being the Servant in perfect love of God and man. For Him that is the only thing in the world that comes with an absolute and unqualified claim. Not even the Law can compare with this supreme obligation. That is not to say that Jesus rejected the Law or that He lightly disregarded any of its commands and prohibitions. It does mean that He did not hesitate to break through its restrictions in the interest of His own task ; and that He reserved the right to criticize freely, not only the oral tradition and the scribal decisions, but even the written Torah itself.

We can see this clearly enough if we take a single example—the Sabbath law.[1] This has the advantage

---

[1] [Cf. Loewe, vol. i, where a detailed suggestive treatment is given to this question on pp. 165–177. ED.]

that it is a matter on which we have a considerable amount of evidence in the Gospels. We can thus obtain a fairly definite picture of the mind of Jesus on this matter. Moreover, from the other side it is to be noted that the Sabbath is the subject of definite commandments in the Torah, and that it has a vast accumulation of traditional material besides. And finally there is clear and ample evidence that the high place taken by the Sabbath was no mere academic dignity grounded in the Torah and fenced by the tradition : it was a place in the hearts of the ordinary people who had given their lives in defence of its sanctity.[1] Among such people Jesus had been brought up—pious, God-fearing Jews to whom His behaviour during the Ministry was a cause of perplexity and distress—and it is not open to us to ascribe His treatment of the Sabbath laws as due either to ignorance or insensitiveness. Indeed, when the relevant stories in the Gospels are carefully examined, it at once appears that the Sabbath rules are, so to speak, broken on principle, and that the principle is that the claims of the Kingdom of God—in other words the exigencies of the Ministry—override the Sabbath rules.

The matter is dealt with in Matt. xii. 5 f., where the argument is put in a form that may be regarded as an attempt to meet and convince the strict upholder of Law and tradition on his own ground. " The priests in the temple profane the sabbath and are guiltless." That is to say, the carrying out of the Temple ritual requires work to be done ; and it is done, on the Sabbath, with impunity. This work is permitted by the principle laid down by the lawyers that positive commandments, for whose performance

[1] 1 Macc. ii. 29–38 ; Josephus, *c. Ap.* i. 209–211.

a definite time is prescribed, override the Sabbath laws in case of a clash. This being granted as common ground, the next step is the application of the Rabbinical principle called *qal wā-ḥōmer* (the argument *a minori ad maius*) : " if it is permissible to break the Sabbath law for the sake of the Temple service, how much more should it be broken for the sake of something greater than the Temple and its ritual. And here it is to be noted that it is *a greater thing* than the Temple that is present (τοῦ ἱεροῦ μεῖζόν ἐστιν ὧδε). Jesus does not set Himself up as an arbitrary potentate claiming to override the Law. He acts in the name and in the interests of something greater than Law and Temple. That something is the Kingdom of God.

The same conclusion can be drawn in another way from the story told in Luke xiii. 10–17. There the nerve of the argument is the claim that the crippled woman has been bound by Satan. It is implied that the Ministry is essentially the warfare of the Kingdom of God against the kingdom of Satan ; and as evil works seven days a week, the counter-measures must be applied on the Sabbath as on other days. The liberating work of the Kingdom of God takes precedence of the Sabbath laws.

It is important to realize what this does not mean. Jesus does not claim to be a greater legislator than Moses, or a more learned lawyer than Hillel. He claims nothing for Himself. He appears as the Servant *par excellence* of the Kingdom of God, and it is for the merciful redemptive work of the kingdom that He demands the fullest scope. If the Law stands in the way of that work, so much the worse for the Law.

Paulinism is not essentially different from the teaching of Jesus on these matters. Paul looks back on the Ministry of Jesus in the light of the Church's Easter faith, and he sees the central claim of Jesus triumphantly vindicated.   Through all the epistles runs the conviction, explicitly stated in such passages as Rom. i. 1–3 or Phil. ii. 6–11, that the work of Jesus, the Ministry, the Passion and Resurrection, all these together mark the decisive irruption of the Divine into history.   For Paul Christ *is* the power and wisdom of God—the rule of God effective in human life, the plan of God fulfilled in history.   The supreme revelation has come, not in a " Thou shalt " but in an " I will," not in God's demand but in His gift.

Consequently the Law must take a secondary place in Paul's account of the matter.   When it comes in, it comes in through the exigencies of controversy with those to whom it was of supreme importance—most notably Paul himself in his pre-Christian days.   The central controversy for the Apostle is not that of Faith and Works, but that between God and Satan.   The Faith and Works controversy has obtained an undue emphasis through our reading of Paul in the light of the soul-strivings of Luther.   In Paulinism the vital question for men is the question how they are to be delivered from the dominion of Sin and Death into what he calls the glorious liberty of the children of God ; from the kingdom of Satan into the Kingdom of God.

Prior to this deliverance man is in subjection to a foreign power ; the reign of Sin and Death over mankind is in full swing (Rom. v. 12–21 ; vi. 12–14) ; men are in a state of abject slavery to Sin (Rom. vi. 6, 16 f., 20, 23 ; vii. 11, 14, 23, 25).[1]   The actual

---

[1] It is to be noted that Sin and Death are treated by Paul as almost personal beings, so that Sin is almost synonymous with Satan.

condition of man *vis-à-vis* the demands of the Law is thus not that of an autonomous being standing between the claims of the Law and the seductions of evil and free to choose which he will obey. He is a subject and slave of Sin, liable to all the consequences that follow from being in that condition. He is in a state of enmity towards God and is himself exposed to God's wrath. The natural man is travelling as fast as his two feet will carry him to perdition.

This desperate condition is universal. Paul deals with it at length in Rom. i. 18–iii. 20, and for the purposes of his discussion he accepts the division of mankind into Jew and Gentile. The wretched state of the Gentiles hardly needs any demonstration. The Jew, on the other side, has the special revelation of the truth which is embodied in the Torah. But, for Paul, the special advantages enjoyed by Israel serve only to aggravate Israel's transgressions. " You only have I known of all the nations of the earth ; therefore I will punish you for all your transgressions." [1] The conclusion of the argument is reached (Rom. iii. 9) when it is shown that all men, Jews as well as Gentiles, are under Sin.[2]

For Paul the Gospel is the account of what God has done to bring this state of things to an end. And be it noted that it is what *God* has done. *Ex hypothesi*, man can do nothing to free himself. He is too deeply enmeshed in the toils of Sin by heredity, environment, and his own acts. The history of salvation is for Paul the history of God's interventions, and above all of

[1] Amos iii. 2.
[2] Paul's explanation of how this state of affairs has come about is given in Rom. v. 12–19, and is based on the story of the Fall as told in Genesis.

His decisive intervention in Christ. In this history there are three turning-points : the promise to Abraham, the giving of the Law, and the fulfilment of the promise in Christ.

(1) *The Promise to Abraham* (Gal. iii. 1–iv. 7 ; Rom. iv).—In laying supreme emphasis on this Paul parts company with Judaism. For Judaism the great thing was the deliverance from Egypt together with the giving of the Law. Paul reverses the emphasis. Judaism would read the patriarchal narratives in the light of Sinai ; Paul insists on looking at Sinai from the standpoint of the promise to Abraham. What we have in Gal. iii. f. and Rom. iv is thus, in a measure, anti-Jewish polemic. And the reason is plain. The Law is a peculiarly Jewish possession. It is a covenant between God and a definite section of mankind. Whereas, according to Paul, the promise to Abraham is universal in its scope ; [1] and a universal remedy is required to meet the universal calamity caused by the Fall. By His dealings with Abraham God definitely commits Himself to the establishment of a new relation with man, universal in its scope, based on God's side on His free grace, on man's side on trust, to be realized in the future. Paul's claim is that God has carried out that contract in Christ, and that the enjoyment of its benefits is there waiting for those who by faith are united to Christ.

This very drastic treatment of the Old Testament story could not, of course, commend itself to orthodox

---

[1] Paul makes much of the fact that the promise was made to Abraham before he was circumcised, i.e. it was made to him as a man and not as the first Jew (Gal. iii. 9–12). From this Paul infers the universal application of the promise to Jew and Gentile alike.

Judaism. For the Rabbis the Law was the charter of God's people. It was, under God, the primary thing, and the view just sketched seems to leave no place for it. But Paul accepted the Old Testament as God's Word, and the giving of the Law was certainly there. What did he make of it ?

(2) *The Giving of the Law.*—The discussion begins in earnest at Gal. iii. 17. Paul starts from the principle that God's promise is His bond. The promise holds the field, and the Law which comes in 430 years later cannot qualify the promise in any way that would make it ineffective. The question naturally arises : then why bring in the Law at all ? Paul offers two main reasons : (*a*) It serves to clarify the moral and religious situation (Gal. iii. 19 ; Rom. iv. 15—where there is no Law there is no transgression). It establishes a rational connexion between acts and their consequences in the moral sphere. It imparts consciousness of sin (Rom. iii. 20). It gives to sinful acts the quality of conscious and deliberate transgression, of doing not merely what is contrary to the will of God, but what we know to be contrary to the will of God. It makes wrong-doing definitely an act of rebellion against God. (*b*) It acts as a stimulus to sin (Rom. vii. 8). In what sense this can be to the credit of the Law is not clear, unless perhaps it were to act as a kind of poultice and bring matters more quickly to a head, that grace and faith might sooner get to work.

As for the Law itself, it is on a different basis from the promise. The promise involves a free gift from God appropriated by faith or trust on man's part. The Law involves a reward or payment on God's part earned by the good behaviour of man (Rom. iv. 4).

What is offered by the grace of God in the promise, and as God's reward in the Law, is the same thing— life (Gal. iii. 11 f.: ὁ δίκαιος ἐκ πίστεως ζήσεται : ὁ ποιήσας αὐτὰ ζήσεται ἐν αὐτοῖς). The weakness of the Law as compared with the promise is, of course, that the condition on which life is offered in the Law is the one condition which man is not in a position to fulfil. All that, in the long run, the Law does is to make abundantly clear that it is the promise and its fulfilment in Christ to which man must look for life. "It conducts men to Christ" is the best that can be said for it.

(3) *The Work of Christ.*—It lies outside the scope of this paper to discuss this subject in any detail. It must suffice to say that the work of Christ as Paul conceives it does for man what he cannot do for himself and what the Law cannot do for him. This achievement is salvation from the condition in which man is into the condition which God wills for him. It can be said that the work of Christ is the work of God, a revelation of God's love, a reconciliation of men to God, a "justification" of men by God. The difference between this and the Law reaches its sharpest and most paradoxical expression in Rom. iv. 5, where Paul describes God as τὸν δικαιοῦντα τὸν ἀσεβῆ, i.e. as doing what the Law forbids [1] and still remaining just Himself (Rom. iii. 26). The Law is superseded as an instrument of salvation, yet retained and main- tained as an expression of the ethical demand of God, which not even He can abrogate without denying Himself. In the Gospel God regards sinful man as righteous while still maintaining the real difference between righteousness and its opposite. Now what is

---

[1] Exod. xxiii. 7 : οὐ δικαιώσεις τὸν ἀσεβῆ.

required in order that a justifying God may Himself be just is that the justified sinner should be a genuinely repentant sinner. The work of Christ may be described as that which makes it possible for sinful men truly to repent. But repentance must be understood in its fullest and deepest sense, a sense in which it means far more than *satisfaction*.

Now repentance in the world of Jesus and Paul and the Rabbis has a deep sense which it scarcely has among the Greeks. For whereas μετανοεῖν in extra-Biblical Greek generally means regret that some particular act has been done or left undone, and so has to do with the details of behaviour rather than with the disposition of the man himself, μετανοεῖν as the equivalent of the Hebrew שוב and μετάνοια as the equivalent of תשׁוּבה do constantly imply a complete change of character and disposition, a turning away from a whole course of behaviour to a different course of behaviour. It is a turning of the whole man from one way to another, a return to God and His obedience from some other attachment.[1]

In the New Testament repentance is of the nature of תשובה—it is a change of the whole man and his inmost disposition, the throwing off of old loyalties and ties to make a new submission of the will to God's will. That is sound Jewish doctrine. Mere confession and remorse is not enough either for Jewish or Christian doctrine on this subject.[2] The essential

---

[1] The essential parts of repentance in Jewish teaching are (*a*) confession of sin and petition for forgiveness, with regret and sorrow ; (*b*) the abandonment of the sin. Where either of these is lacking, the repentance is not a complete repentance (תשובה שלימה), but is a hypocritical repentance, which, if persisted in, will end by destroying the possibility of genuine repentance (Billerbeck, *Komm.*, i. 170).　　　　[2] Cf. 2 Cor. vii. 9 f.

difference between Judaism and Christianity is not
that they have different ideas about repentance. They
have not. It is rather that for Judaism repentance is
something which man ought to do ; for Christianity
it is something which man can do because Christ has
made it possible. The difference stares us in the face
when we compare the preaching of John the Baptist,
as noble a representative as one could imagine of the
old order, with the formulation of the primitive
Christian kerygma.[1] In the one case repentance is an
obligation, in the other it is a gift.

Here we are brought back to the point that in
Paul's view of the matter man is incapable of
responding to a command to repent in this full sense
of the word. He can regret his faults and feel
remorse ; but he is enslaved to sin and cannot break
free from the chains that bind him. Only by an act
of God can he be liberated. And for Paul Christ is
the liberator who makes possible the repentance that
is necessary if man is to be justified. How ? For
Paul three elements seem to be involved : (a) In the
life, death, and resurrection of Jesus there is given
a new revelation of God's nature as one who is ready
to seek and save the lost (Rom. v. 8). It becomes
possible for man to turn to God with real trust,
because in Christ it is made certain that God is
waiting to receive him graciously. (b) In the death
and resurrection there is given a real victory over the
powers of evil that hold man in servitude.[2] (c) The

---

[1] Mark i. 4: κηρύσσων βάπτισμα μετανοίας εἰς ἄφεσιν
ἁμαρτιῶν. Acts v. 31 : τοῦτον (sc. Ἰησοῦν) ὁ θεὸς ἀρχηγὸν καὶ
σωτῆρα ὕψωσε τῇ δεξιᾷ αὐτοῦ, τοῦ δοῦναι μετάνοιαν τῷ Ἰσραὴλ
καὶ ἄφεσιν ἁμαρτιῶν.

[2] Cf. Aulén, Christus Victor, pp. 82–89.

effect on the individual is twofold. There is created in him the confidence that he can approach God ; and the things in the man himself, which hinder him from coming to God and make him unwilling to part from his sins, are removed or nullified.

The upshot of it all is that " what the law could not do, in that it was weak through the flesh, God, sending his own Son in the likeness of flesh of sin, and for sin, condemned sin in the flesh : that the ordinance of the law might be fulfilled in us, who walk not after the flesh, but after the spirit " (Rom. viii. 3 f.). The Law as an instrument of salvation is ineffective and is superseded : as a moral requirement it remains in force, though no longer as bare demand backed by sanctions.

The situation is changed in that Paul substitutes for acts of obedience to the Law, what he calls the " fruit of the spirit " (Gal. v. 22), the " fruit of light " (Eph. v. 9), or the " fruit of righteousness " (Phil. i. 11). Here the word " fruit " seems to be chosen deliberately in order to suggest that the good deeds of the believer are characterized by a certain spontaneity. They are the natural outcome of a transformed nature rather than the laborious attempt to conform to an external code. The good things that the Law requires are still to be done, but the motive and driving force behind the actions is something more than moral striving after obedience. The difference between Saul of Tarsus and Paul the Apostle is that Saul would have said, " If you do not fulfil the Law, you will not be saved," while Paul would say, " If you do not fulfil the Law, you have not been saved."

But here again there is a difference. Fulfilment of the Law for Saul the Pharisee meant exact obedience to each and every precept, with no right to question any or to reckon one as more important than another. For Paul the Apostle the whole Law is summed up in this : thou shalt love thy neighbour as thyself (Gal. v. 14). This drastic simplification does not by any means allow the concrete detailed requirements of duty to evaporate in mawkish sentiment. On the contrary, the letters of Paul teem with definite moral instructions and exhortations. The meaning of " love thy neighbour as thyself " is construed in many different contexts. But it is that one single and fundamental principle that is being applied all the time. And the very fact that it is the principle " Thou shalt love " that has to be applied means that in every case the act must be in some measure a creative original reaction to the situation. It can never be mere obedience to precept. The beginning of right relations with one's neighbour is to see in him one for whom Christ died (Rom. xiv. 15).

Consequently, though it is true to say that the Law expresses the demands of a holy and righteous God upon men—and that is substantially what Paul means when he says that the Law is holy, and the commandment holy and just and good (Rom. vii. 12)—yet it is not the whole truth nor the last word on the subject, even for Paul. For the final rule of behaviour in the New Testament is the imitation of Christ, ultimately the imitation of God [1] (Matt. v. 48 ; Luke vi. 36 ; 1 Cor. xi. 1 ; Eph. v. 1 ; 1 Thess. i. 6). That is to say, the standard of human behaviour is set by an act of God rather than by a mere demand of God. That act of God is identified with the Ministry of Jesus.

[1] Be it noted that the God in question is the God of Israel and not the God of the Greeks.

Here Jesus and Paul are fundamentally in agreement. For Jesus sees the " finger of God " in the Ministry and the will of God behind all that He undertakes ; and that is the secret of the " authority " (ἐξουσία) which caused so much amazement, and the justification of His breaches of the Law. Paul equally sees in the Ministry and its sequel the act of God : Christ is the Θεοῦ δύναμιν—God's mighty act (1 Cor. i. 24).

This means that the pattern for men's imitation is given in a person and a life rather than in a set of precepts. And this is seen to be inevitable. The essence of the New Testament teaching on this matter is that the real demand of God upon man cannot be revealed adequately by a command but only by a gift from God. By what He gives He shows most clearly what He requires ; and by what He gives He makes it possible to begin to do what He requires.

There is thus no place of final authority left for the Law in the New Testament. As a means of salvation it is declared to be ineffective, a mere stop-gap, rendered obsolete by the salvation wrought by God in Christ. As a revelation of the moral demands of God it is declared to be superseded by the better revelation given in the life and teaching of Jesus. All that can be said for the Law is said by Paul : ὥστε ὁ νόμος παιδαγωγὸς ἡμῶν γέγονεν εἰς Χριστόν (Gal. iii. 24) ; and it is not too much to say that this conclusion merely makes explicit what is already implied in the Ministry of Jesus itself. To the two questions : What does God offer to man ? and What does God require of man ? the New Testament returns one answer : the Life of Christ.

VII

LAW AND RELIGION IN ISLAM

BY

H. A. R. GIBB

VII

IN giving a place in this series to Islam, it is perhaps
necessary to point out that we are not introducing
a totally unrelated Eastern culture. Islam is not an
Eastern religion except in a relative or geographical
sense. The truly Eastern religions and civilizations
are those of India and China. Islam is only the
Eastern branch of our own civilization, of that fairly
homogeneous group of cultures and religions that
embrace Western Asia and Europe. The springs upon
which it drew, and the elements which went to make
up its spiritual and intellectual life, were to a large
extent the same as those of mediæval Judaism and of
Christianity ; Islam is co-heir with ourselves to Greek
culture and Hebrew religion, and is of our own kin.
But as co-heirs and kinsmen will use their patrimony
and order their lives in very different fashions, so too
the course of spiritual and intellectual development
in two kindred societies will follow divergent paths.
And this supplies a further reason why Islam should
come into the series ; for if we trace the lines along
which the Islamic culture developed from a starting-
point very close to our own, they may by contrast

[1] The reader is referred to E. Rosenthal's *Islam* in vol. ii,
pp. 147 ff., especially pp. 167 ff., for a discussion of the relations
between Jewish and Islamic Law.

illustrate for us more clearly the character of our own development.

But quite apart from this, the Islamic system has, in our chosen field of Law in relation to Religion, an independent and proper value of its own. It has been pointed out by Dr. George Sarton that it was in Islam that the first attempt was made to combine the cultural traditions derived from the Greeks and the Hebrews. Like all first attempts it was not a very successful combination, but rather a co-ordination, in which the two traditions were confined to separate spheres, rarely competing and interacting. From the Greek tradition derive the mathematical, scientific, medical and philosophical activities of the Muslims of the Middle Ages ; from the Hebraic derive the religious sciences in the narrower sense. It is true that Greek philosophical ideas forced their way into theology and at length reshaped it altogether ; but into the practical science of religious duties they gained no entrance.

Now in Islam, Law, as we shall see, was a part of the science of religious duties. It is a fact of great importance that the body of Roman Law, and even its basic principles, seem to have been entirely unknown to the Muslim jurists. Local infiltrations of Roman-Byzantine Law undoubtedly took place, but these borrowings could not and did not affect their conceptions and methods. Consequently, Islamic Law in its theoretical aspect derives from what I have called the Hebraic tradition. But this is perhaps a misleading name ; for this " tradition " is only to a very limited extent derived from Judaism. The ethical monotheism of Islam, both in Muḥammad's own preaching and in its later development, is derived from and influenced by both Judaism and Eastern Christianity ; but—and this is the important thing—the legacy of these forerunners was worked over and reinterpreted in a spirit neither Jewish nor Christian, but specifically Islamic.[1] And the result was to produce a system of law which stands in a class by itself, as the most fully and logically developed example of theocratic law.

The statement just made seems to call for some definition of the " specifically Islamic spirit." But this is much too lengthy and too difficult a task to attempt here. It is a spirit that can be more easily grasped by observing its effects than by any kind of formal definition, the more so that the elements with which it operates are common to all the Western monotheistic religions. What distinguishes it from the others is rather the relative emphasis which it lays upon these elements, so that the resulting combinations differ widely from those more familiar to us in Judaism and Christianity. For our present purposes, the two elements most strongly emphasized are the absolute sovereignty of God and the brotherhood of all Believers. On these twin pillars—one dogmatic, one ethical—rests the entire structure of Islamic Law, and from their dogmatic and ethical content are derived, by a process of strict logic, its specific provisions. They are explicitly set down in two fundamental texts of the Koran : Sūra 45, v. 17 : " We have set thee upon an Highway of command, do thou therefore follow it " (from which is taken the technical term for the Islamic Law, *Sharī'a*, " Highway "), and Sūra 49, v. 10 : " The Believers are Brethren ; bring about then a reconciliation between your two brothers

[1] [Cf. Rosenthal, vol. ii, p. 149.—ED.]

[or it might be translated " bring your two brothers to agree upon their mutual interest "] and fear ye God, that haply ye shall attain mercy."

Yet on these two pillars might be erected very different structures, and there is still a third element in the " Islamic spirit " which determined the kind of structure actually raised. This is that bent of the Islamic mind—what Whitehead would call its " particular temperament "—sometimes described, rather unhappily, as " traditionalism " or " conservatism," but which is rather a synthetic inclination. By this I mean that characteristic effort to hold fast to old and well-tried ways, which have been accepted as good, and to assimilate to them all newer problems, methods and activities, whether indigenous or foreign. The Muslim scholar seldom reaches out boldly to grasp a new conception, but advances towards it with infinite caution, testing every inch of the way, so that, when at length he reaches it, it fits easily into the place which has already been prepared for it within the framework of accepted ideas.

It is a belief still widely held, even amongst well-read people, that Islamic Law was laid down immutably once and for all by Muḥammad in the Koran. If this phrase is properly understood, there is some truth in it, but not in the literal sense in which it is commonly taken. The Koran is not a law-book, though it contains legal materials, nor did Muḥammad formulate a very large number of legal decisions. The Koran is a hand-book of religious doctrine, precept, and practice. In our eyes it is a collection of Muḥammad's discourses, but to all Muslims it is the explicit and directly inspired word of God Himself. And the letter and spirit of its teachings may be summed up for us in the familiar words of the Hebrew prophet Micah : " He hath showed thee, O man, what is good ; and what doth the Lord require of thee, but to do justly, and to love mercy, and to walk humbly with thy God ? " (vi. 8).

The Koran contains therefore not the formulation, but the basis of Islamic Law. For to the Muslim jurists, religion and law are indivisible, although law and theology are by no means one and the same. Law is the external aspect of religion ; that is to say, it is the attempt to give formal shape and definition to the multiple relations existing between man and God, and man and man. Or, to put it in the words of a famous Muslim jurist : " The science of Law is the knowledge of the rights and duties whereby man is enabled to observe right conduct in this life, and to prepare himself for the world to come." From this follow two important consequences, which stand out at the first glance as distinguishing features of law in Islam, as contrasted with the kind of law which Christendom inherited from Rome. The first is the width of the field which it covers, since it must take in all kinds of relationships, even including those which we are accustomed to regard as outside the concern of law, as, for example, the performance of religious duties and the giving of alms. The second is the spirit by which its judgments are animated. For if the inner aspect of these relations is religion, the outer aspect cannot be other than ethical ; and in fact Islamic Law is even more firmly founded upon ethical principle than is Islamic theology. In framing its definitions, therefore, the ethical aspect is paramount ; and in no case may the legal judgment conflict with it. Hence, for example, Islamic Law refuses to admit of

legal rights which may be exercised to the detriment
of oneself or of one's neighbour, such as to practise
usury in any sense whatsoever, or even to do as one
likes with one's own property. The Roman *jus utendi
et abutendi* is regarded as the very negation of law, and
to this day a spendthrift is liable to find himself placed
under legal restraint on the motion of his putative
heirs. A still more remarkable example is offered by
the following case : if a Muslim and a non-Muslim
contest the guardianship of a minor, the Muslim
claiming him as his slave, the non-Muslim as his son ;
then, say the jurists, the presumption lies in favour of
the non-Muslim, because it is in the interest of the boy
that he should be free. Above all, the Koran explicitly and on all occasions stresses the doctrine of
" forgiveness," that is to say, of renouncing or refusing
to take advantage of one's strict due for the sake of
the general well-being. Justice remains, but religion
demands that it shall be tempered with mercy, or
even, in the relations between man and man, replaced
by mercy.

Nevertheless, the law must be explicitly formulated,
even if at some cost to ethical ideals, and to this task
generations of Muslim jurists bent their energies. It is
unnecessary to give more than a general description
of their principles and methods here, since the
technical details are too complicated to be compressed
into a few paragraphs, and in any case they hardly
concern our subject.

The fundamental proposition is that Good, in the
absolute sense, is not a thing which can be rationally
ascertained nor reached by the agreement of a
majority of men. Absolute Good is known only to
God, and can be made known to men only through

Revelation. " Rational systems of Law," says Ibn Khaldūn, " are blameworthy, because they are the product of speculation without the light of God." " *He* hath showed thee, O man, what is good " ; consequently, the foundation of law cannot be other than the divine precepts and prohibitions contained in the Koran.

But, as we have already seen, the Koran is not a law-book, and though in the Muslim view it contains the principles of all law, the number of judgments which it actually formulates is very small. In order to supplement these, the natural—indeed the only possible—source (at least in the first instance) is offered by the judgments and practice of the inspired Prophet. For Muslim dogma asserts that in all his sayings and doings which are not recorded in the Koran, Muhammad was acting under " tacit inspiration." The statements of these sayings and doings, narrated through generations of pious transmitters, and under the control of a fairly rigorous criticism, form a second infallible source. These, of course, cover a very much wider field. Yet, even so, a very large number of legal problems, especially those which arose after Muhammad's death, remained to be solved. But it was held, by the great majority of the Muslim community at least, that the Prophetic office was not inherited by Muhammad's successors ; consequently, no further direct sources of law existed.

To escape from this dilemma, the Muslim jurists admitted, as additional " sources," two further principles. Although Prophetic inspiration, in the strict sense, had ceased, it was held that the consensus of the Muslim community (expressed, of course, through the consensus of the jurists [1]) was, in a sense, inspired and so also infallible. " My Community," Muḥammad is reported to have said, " will never agree upon an error." The other principle should more exactly be called a " method," not a " source," since it consisted in trying to find a solution for new problems by analogy with established judgments, where it could be shown that the factors or elements in the two cases were similar and produced similar effects. If consensus and analogy should happen to conflict, consensus is of course the stronger. When, for example, the use of coffee began to spread in the sixteenth and seventeenth centuries, the jurists at first almost unanimously took the view that, since coffee was a stimulant and harmful if taken to excess, it was analogous to wine-drinking, and therefore unlawful and punishable with the same penalties as were applied to wine-drinkers. But analogy was powerless against consensus, and to this day coffee is freely consumed by even the strictest and most puritan of Muslim sectaries.

Consensus, in fact, although in theory it is given only a very limited rôle, plays a decisive part in almost every phase of Islamic Law. In the very early days, before the Muslim jurists had worked out the principles and methods of their science, there was a tendency in certain circles to pronounce decisions based upon personal interpretation of legal principles rather than to search for precedents in the practice of Muḥammad and his successors. But consensus stepped in and ruled that a valid precedent, once established by authentic tradition, was immutable, and that personal interpretation must be confined to

[1] [See, on this point, Rosenthal, vol. ii, p. 180.—ED.]

matters not so decided. It went further, and ruled that once a decision on any of these outstanding matters was given by a jurist of recognized standing, and accepted by other jurists, it too formed an immutable precedent. Consequently, the scope of personal interpretation was rapidly narrowed down in successive generations, until by the fourth century after Muḥammad it was generally held that all valid precedents had now been established, and that later jurists were not at liberty to do more than interpret and apply them within narrow limits.

It should be clear from this that consensus plays a dual rôle : on the one hand opening the door to modifications, on the other tending to stereotype the structure and content of Islamic Law once and for all. Sometimes, therefore, it may seem to speak with two voices, as, for instance, in the question of admitting the principles of " Expediency " and " the Greatest Good " in the determination of difficult problems not fully covered by the recognized sources. For while there is certainly no general acceptance of their legality in theory, the second at least is admitted in practice by all schools in certain cases.

It was, however, precisely because of this dual function of *Ijmāʿ*, as the consensus of jurists is called, that Islamic Law remained a working and workable system. To some readers, perhaps, it may seem curious that nothing has been said up to now about legislation by what we are accustomed to think of as the sovereign state. The answer is that the state was not sovereign, and had no legislative powers except in matters of military and civil administration. For the rest it was itself merely the executive of the law, which it could not alter and to which it was itself

subject. This is the most striking proof of the strength
of the theocratic conception. The law was laid
down by jurists, independent of either Caliph or
Sultan, and often in opposition to them. It had
merely to be formulated by the jurists to become
valid ; it had no need of formal promulgation by the
civil authorities, nor could the Caliph deny its validity,
though he might not always act in accordance
with it.

Such a state of affairs would have been impossible
unless the law itself had been a uniform and living
organism, with an inherent power of development and
the support of an authority even higher than the state.
The doctrine of consensus guaranteed its uniformity
and continuity, and gave it the power to develop ;
and the doctrine of divine inspiration gave it executive
force. Thus for twelve centuries the fabric of the law
maintained itself supreme and homogeneous from end
to end of the Islamic world, unaffected by wars and
revolutions, by the rise and fall of dynasties and the
personal idiosyncrasies of autocratic rulers. From
time to time its administration might be hindered or
confused, its prerogatives flouted, its representatives
corrupt—but there was no other law and could be no
other law in the eyes of the Muslim peoples. No
Caliph or Sultan ever dared to supplant it, and even
when they began to supplement it they were careful
to gain the approval of legal authority for their
enactments.

But it is time for us now to look at the actual
content of this law. Two principles are combined
in it, one rigid, the other flexible, both derived from
religious axioms. The rigid principle is that which
insists upon the literal and exact observance of the

positive injunctions contained in the Koran or laid down by Muḥammad, and the avoidance of prohibited actions. With these there can be no tampering. The flexible principle is derived from the axiom : " The general rule is permissibility," and allows a wide latitude in regard to actions not expressly prescribed or forbidden. This latitude is circumscribed in greater or less degree by the interpretations of successive generations of jurists, based upon the methods already described and evolved to meet individual cases as they arose. But these interpretations take in general the form of a discussion, ending with the statement of the resulting decision. The doctrine of consensus, as we have seen, gives all such decisions as are generally accepted the force of binding precedents.[1]

It does not, however, exclude the possibility that different jurists with equal qualifications may have come to different decisions on the same point ; and thus a number of " schools " arose in the first centuries of Islam, each accepting the decisions of different teachers. But here again consensus intervened in a manner which is characteristically Islamic. It first operated to reduce gradually the number of divergent " schools," and then accepted those that remained as all equally valid. Moreover, it succeeded in reducing the divergences between the " schools " to matters mostly of minor moment, so that the essential uniformity of the law was not endangered. And, what is still more striking, this applies not only to the law-schools of the orthodox majority, but also to those of the Shi'ites and other dissident factions,

[1] [Note the striking similarity in Judaism. Cf. Mishnah and Gemara in the Talmud. See *below*, Rosenthal, p. 185.—ED.]

although all of these rejected in theory the principle
of consensus.

Moreover, just as the jurists showed a wise humanity
in tolerating minor divergences, so also there was
wisdom, though perhaps unconscious in this instance,
in the fluidity of their formulation of the law. It was
not until the nineteenth century that, under Western
influences, the first attempts were made to codify the
law in a rigid form.   Until then it remained as we have
seen it, a complex of fixed rules and general principles,
the application of which is worked out in a vast number
of discussions and accepted precedents, embodied in
a literature running into thousands of volumes.

In the standard text-books these rules and precedents are generally expressed in legal form : if
such-and-such actions are done, then the legal consequences are so-and-so. But all these maxims are
based on the underlying ethical or religious principle,
which is concerned less with the legal consequences
than with the valuation of the actions themselves in
terms of Good and Evil. These can all be classified
under five heads : compulsory, recommended, in-
different, disapproved, and prohibited.   In this complex of Thou shalt, Thou shouldest, Thou mayest,
Thou oughtest not, Thou shalt not, penalties in the
legal sense can attach only to omission of the first
and commission of the last. The penalties themselves
are generally similar to those in other systems of law,
though in a number of cases the only penalty laid
down is a religious one—that is to say, it lies in the
public dishonour attaching to the action. At the same
time a wide latitude is left in these cases to the judge
to determine how far it may be supplemented by
civil penalties.

The jurists were, in fact, conscious throughout that their function was that of maintaining the ethical standards of Islam, as laid down by Muḥammad and his immediate followers. This needed constant watchfulness to hold the balance between opposite extremes. On the one hand they had to resist the tendency of the rulers towards secularizing the law and its administration ; and, even as amongst themselves, to guard against the danger of externalizing the law, by emphasizing the letter and neglecting the spirit. On the other hand there were the extreme pietists of the early generations, who would have made any development of law impossible ; and in later times there was a strong antinomian tendency in some mystical circles, to disregard formal law and claim that the spirit alone mattered. That the jurists succeeded on the whole in keeping an even balance can hardly, I think, be doubted ; although perhaps as time went on, and particularly in more recent centuries, we may discern amongst the official administrators of the law a certain hardening in the direction of literalism.

There remains, however, one very important question. However admirable this legal structure may be in its principles and deductions, to what extent was it effective in practice ? Was it as supreme in fact as it claimed to be in theory, and were its definitions and decisions accepted and applied in every range of Muslim society ? The answer is neither a straight yes nor a plain no. The subject is full of difficulties, and in addition its investigation has scarcely gone as yet beyond the first stages. What follows consequently cannot be more than a personal interpretation, based rather on general indications than on exhaustive research.

Islamic jurisprudence is firmly based upon realities, but the structure raised by the jurists was largely theoretical in the first instance. This can clearly be seen by going through a translation of any of the standard treatises. The method of the jurists was to elaborate the widest possible variety of " type " cases, even to the point of absurdity, and to formulate their decisions on these in the light of their general principles. Many cases did, of course, arise in practice, but the formulation of the law was independent of the existence of actual cases.

But this is only the outer shell of the law. It is a characteristic of almost all Muslim institutions that the external form conceals more often than it reveals the inner reality. Yet the two are very closely related, and when the real facts, as we should call them, are investigated and understood, their relationship to the external or theoretical structure gradually becomes apparent and gives to it a significance and a natural *raison d'être* which had not hitherto been appreciated.

So it is here too. What we see in the external formulation of Islamic Law is an ideal structure. The foundations upon which it is based, and more especially the doctrine of Divine Revelation, inevitably lead to the conception of " absolute justice," framed in general and therefore theoretical terms, in abstraction from personalities and confusing issues. The jurists themselves were well aware of this, and while they upheld the absolute validity of their solutions to all problems of human relations, they realized that, in the handling of practical cases, the abstract ideal must reckon with the concrete facts.

This was made easier and more natural for them by the fact that Islamic scholars rarely allowed their ideal concepts to override the human factors—all the more so that this was (and still is) precisely the charge which they brought against Christianity. In our present field, in particular, alongside their conviction of the divine revelation of the *Sharī'a*, they had inherited from Muḥammad and the Arabian past a second cardinal principle, that of *inṣāf*, as it was called. In some respects *inṣāf* resembles the English conception of Equity, but differs from Equity in that instead of superseding the original law it determines the method of its application. It is fundamentally concerned with persons and specific cases ; it cannot be theoretical and abstract, like justice. *Inṣāf* means to reconcile conflicting interests by a solution which all the parties concerned accept as satisfying their sense of fairness, or, more briefly, to give every man his due. This was, and remains to this day, the basic principle of Bedouin justice, and, as we have seen, it is explicitly taken up and made mandatory in the Koranic text : " Bring about a reconciliation between your two brothers."

But like all other Arabian customs taken up into Islām it was profoundly modified by acquiring an ethical aspect. The verse just quoted continues, it will be remembered : " And fear ye God, that haply ye shall obtain mercy." Henceforward, therefore, there was a third party to every case, which also had to be satisfied and given its due, namely the Divine Law. We may sum up the situation broadly thus : in theory, the Divine Law supplied a solution for every case, but its solutions were " type " solutions which had in practice to be applied to specific cases by adopting the principles of *inṣāf*. Thus its impersonal precepts were brought into harmony with the intensely personal conception of justice to which the Eastern peoples have always clung. Our familiar personification of justice as blindfolded is repugnant to them ; on the contrary, they laid stress on " intelligence," the Arabic word for which simply means "sight" or " insight," as an essential quality in the *qāḍī* or " decider," whose duty it was to apply the law in the spirit of *inṣāf*.

The same principle underlies a further peculiar development of Islamic Law, the so-called *ḥiyal* or " subterfuges," which are openly admitted by the most widely recognized " school " (the Ḥanafite) and somewhat more grudgingly by the other " schools." This has often been pointed to by critics as an example not only of juristic casuistry, but as a moral weakness detracting from the high ethico-religious ideals of the law. That it has been abused by unscrupulous jurists cannot be denied, but its central purpose was quite a different one. It was found that cases sometimes arose in which to apply the strict letter of the law would result in a decision contrary to the ethical principle of *inṣāf*; and in such a conflict the judge was at liberty, without injury to his conscience, to take advantage of any loophole to satisfy the demands of equity. The Koran itself sanctions the practice ; for in reference to the legend that Job, in a moment of anger, swore to give his wife a hundred stripes, the command is given to him (Sūra 38, v. 43) : " Take in thine hand a bundle [of rushes], and strike therewith, and forswear not thyself."

The further categories of *ḥiyal* admitted by the Ḥanafite school come closer to our " legal fictions," with this difference, that they do not replace the normal rule of law but merely permit certain local deviations. The right of pre-emption, for example, is, under given conditions, an absolute rule of Islamic Law, but as applied to certain forms of urban property may be injurious in its effects. In these cases the Ḥanafite lawyers were furnished with means to set aside its strict application and adapt it to local circumstances.

Although by such methods as these the law became adaptable to all practical problems, it still remained a serious problem to ensure and safeguard its application. Islam extended over a wide area containing numerous peoples and groups who already possessed a law, either written or traditional. The Muslim jurists speak of all such pre-existing law as 'āda, " custom," or 'urf, " what is done," and almost unanimously, of course (in view of their first principles), take the line that 'urf or 'āda is inferior law which should be replaced by the Sharī'a.

But the structure of Islamic society was such that 'urf or 'āda could not easily be suppressed. It is true that in the course of centuries Islamic influences permeated and reshaped all of the older societies which had been absorbed ; yet, almost down to our own time, what we call Islamic society was not a homogeneous and organically unified whole but a co-ordination of vast numbers of small groups, local, industrial, and professional. Each little group was largely self-governing and autonomous, in the sense that its internal affairs were regulated by a code of customs administered by its own officers. It was comparatively rarely that qāḍīs or official jurists were called in to deal with these matters at all, although their competence was generally recognized in such matters as personal status and inheritance.

M

A great deal of this customary law, of course, did not conflict with the *Sharī'a*, and where local usages were in conformity with the principle of *inṣāf* (as in the industrial guilds, for example), the legists, on the general principle of " permissibility," rarely interfered. But many particulars, on the other hand, did conflict with the theoretical demands of the *Sharī'a*, and the relentless pressure brought to bear on these points over a long period of centuries is one of the most remarkable features of Islamic juristic activity. Having the type of perfect law clearly before their mental vision, the jurists strove consistently to bring the actual practice into conformity with their ideal.

This task—as indeed the whole operation of adapting the *Sharī'a* to particular cases and situations—was the business of a special class of jurists, distinct from the practising judges, and known as *muftīs*. A *muftī* is a lawyer to whom specific cases are referred, and who, after investigating the precedents and circumstances, embodies his decision in a *fatwā*. There is a whole Arabic literature of *fatwās*, sometimes descriptive and temperate, sometimes phrased in tones of bitter criticism. A considerable number of these works, some of them voluminous, have been published, but the subject as a whole has been very little studied so far. Until this is done, we shall remain very much in the dark as to the details of this protracted task of adjustment and reshaping of customary law.[1]

But the general results are plain enough, and we can see where the jurists failed and where they were successful. Those groups which were powerful enough to withstand their pressure—and this included practi-

[1] [Cf. Rosenthal, *below*, on the *Responsa* of the mediæval Rabbis, the Geonim and their successors, pp. 177 ff.—ED.]

cally all the governing and military classes—were able to do pretty much as they pleased, within limits. And so it came about that the whole administrative organization, including the levying of taxation and what is known as the Islamic feudal system, set the principles of the jurists at nought and followed an evolution of its own, often very far removed from the spirit of Islamic Law. Only the Ottoman Sultans made an effort to adapt their system to some extent to the rules laid down by the jurists, although they too followed the practice of entrusting a good deal of jurisdiction in civil and penal cases to lay officers applying Sultanian regulations, the forerunners of the modern civil and penal codes in Muslim countries.

Amongst the majority of other groups, however, including the industrial, agricultural, professional, and to a lesser degree the commercial classes, the devoted labours of the jurists gained in the end a very substantial measure of success. Some of the more remote groups, such as the Berbers in the mountainous regions of North-West Africa, and the Indonesians in Java and Sumatra, or relatively recent converts, as for example in India, have retained to this day elements of customary law that conflict with the *Sharī'a*, but these and many other minor contradictions do not detract from the magnitude of the achievement. A conception which had the power to make its influence felt throughout such a vast and heterogeneous section of mankind, and to remould its outlook and ways of life in very large measure, deserves at least our attention and respect.

That as a system of law it was not perfect goes without saying. Yet it can face with equanimity many of the criticisms brought against it. It is objected, for example, that it left no room for the application of philosophic ideas to the bases of law. And in fact, although much of Arabic philosophical literature is devoted to the problem of reconciling the Islamic doctrine of a divinely revealed *Sharī'a* with the Greek doctrine of the Lawmaker, the philosophers, so far as I know, show little disposition to deal with the question of Law *ab initio* or in practice.[1] The jurists, likewise, as we have seen, are shy of appealing to external principles such as "Utility" or "the Greatest Good" in support of their decisions, and seek rather to found their arguments upon such accepted texts as lead to the desired end.

Yet just as the apparently static and literalist character of its enactments in reality conceals a process of slow adaptation, so it is clear that a sufficiently general change of view in fundamental matters can be accommodated to Koranic doctrine under pressure from consensus. Although orthodox Islam discourages the idea of change, and the necessity for something like universal acceptance before any accommodation can be made seems to set up an almost impassable barrier, here again the external forms may prove misleading. Orthodox theology has, for example, always rejected any mechanical theory of causation, but the doctrine of the immutable "custom" of God, *sunnat Allāh*, provided Muslim thinkers with quite as stable grounds for the linking of cause and effect. And it must be remembered that the apparent unchangeableness of the law has served to prevent the far greater danger of arbitrary legislation by secular rulers ; while even at the present day

[1] [See also the discussion of this point in mediæval Jewish philosophy, *below*, pp. 196, 200 ff.—ED.]

it stands in the way of hasty improvisation and ensures that the existing basis is not abandoned until the new basis is well established.

A more serious criticism, possibly, from the Western jurist's point of view is that the Islamic legal structure is neither fully rationalized—being rather an attempt to rationalize elements many of which, being either ethical or traditional, are non-rational—nor is it wholly consistent. The answer here would be, I think, that an abstract conception of rational law is a false conception—or rather a partial conception, derived from the Romans—and that justice, when divested of ethical and personal considerations and erected into a system, may be law but is no longer justice.

For at the roots of Muslim thought on law, as in all other intellectual activities in Islam, there lies a deep vein of mysticism. That " mystical influence," which Western observers regard as an irrational impediment to the development of Muslim ideas along lines which seem to themselves so axiomatic, is precisely the element which a better understanding of its nature may show to be their most valuable element. The real is always mysterious, and it is the rational concept which is an abstraction from reality. The Muslim jurists themselves fell into the same pit in their endeavour to develop a legal scholasticism, and all their paraphernalia of " roots of law " are intellectual constructions which veil the reality. But the reality itself was there, in the mystical intuition of Muḥammad, and the very firmness of their hold upon it prevented it from being lost in the web of scholastic discussion. It could not fail to guide them, moreover, in their practical constructions, with the result that their systems, for all that may be urged against them on the score of casuistry and formalism, preserved the recognizable features of a socio-religious ideal in which justice is the servant and not the master of men.

Seen in this light, the fact that the Muslim jurists escaped the influence of Roman Law gains a fresh significance. For the conflict of the two conceptions is fundamental. At the present day, the invasion of the Islamic world by Western ideas has brought with it Western conceptions of law, of codification, and of judicial procedure. Apart altogether from the encroachments of Civil Law upon the domain formerly reserved to it, the administration of the *Sharī'a* has acquired something of the impersonality of Western law, the jurists are considering the possibility of drawing up regular codes, and a *shar'ī* legal profession has sprung up in imitation of European advocates and barristers. But since all these features are foreign to the principles and inner reason of Islamic Law, they are destructive of precisely those elements which gave it its peculiar value. The result has been to throw the whole system into confusion and disrepute, and where this development has gone farthest it is in danger of breaking down altogether. With the ultimate consequences of a breakdown of Islamic Law it is not our place to deal here, but the present conditions serve to bring out more clearly how much the mediæval culture of Islam was shaped by the conception of human relations which it inherited from its founder. To him, as to his followers, any form of dualism was absolutely to be rejected. A man's conduct is ultimately determined by his beliefs as to the nature and governance of the universe ; therefore the rules which govern social relations cannot be divorced from the complex of religious ideas. The corollary that, since the ultimate sanctions of the *Sharīʿa* are religious, it is only for Muslims that it can possess absolute validity, they fully accepted. Jews and Christians should normally, of course, be governed by their own law ; although, since Islam was the final and perfect Revelation, it was open to them to accept its rulings voluntarily. The ideal of a single secular law, like the Roman *Jus Naturale* or *Jus Gentium*, embracing the adherents of different religious communities, could only be an impious illusion. Consequently, while the religious basis of law widened the confessional breach, the *Sharīʿa* was not only the most powerful agency of external unity within the Muslim fold, but was responsible also for the extraordinary degree of inner unity which distinguishes the men of the Islamic civilization. As thought and life were governed by the same ideas, there is a consistency and wholeness in their intellectual and social activity, a serenity of conviction which, however unpropitious to progress, as we have somewhat confidently understood it in the past, is nevertheless the key to that good living which is true culture.

SHORT BIBLIOGRAPHY

MACDONALD, D. B. : *Development of Muslim Theology, Jurisprudence, and Constitutional Theory* (London, 1903, and reprints). Valuable for general background.

JUYNBOLL, TH. W. : *Handbuch des islamischen Gesetzes* (Leiden, 1910).

SANTILLANA, D. : (1) *Istituzioni di diritto musulmana*, vol. i (Rome, 1926 ; vol. ii in the press). Good discussion of principles.

(2) " Law and Society " in *The Legacy of Islam* (Oxford, 1931).

SCHACHT, J. : *G. Bergsträsser's Grundzüge des islamischen Rechts* (Berlin, 1935). Concise survey of legal structure.

168 LAW AND RELIGION IN ISLAM

Morand, M. : *Introduction à l'Étude du Droit musulman algérien* (Algiers, 1921). Valuable for the practical aspects of Islamic Law.

Goldziher, I. : *Vorlesungen über den Islam* (Heidelberg, 1925).

Vesey-Fitzgerald, S. : *Muhammadan Law* (London, 1931).

Baillie, N. B. E. : *A Digest of Moohummudan Law*, 2 vols. (London, 1875–77).

Guillaume, A. : " Philosophy and Theology " in *The Legacy of Islam*.

Levy, R. : *An Introduction to the Sociology of Islam*, vol. ii, chap. iii : " Usage, Custom and Secular Law under Islam " (London, 1933).

Schacht, J. : " Qānūn und Šarīʿa im heutigen Aegypten," in *Der Islam*, vol. xx, pp. 209 *sqq.* ; revised translation, " L'évolution moderne du Droit musulman en Égypte," in *Mélanges Maspéro*, vol. iii (Cairo, 1935).

Rosenthal, E. : " Islam " in *Judaism and Christianity*, vol. ii (London, 1937).

Encyclopædia of Islam : Article " Sharīʿa " and numerous other articles under separate titles.

VIII
MEDIÆVAL JUDAISM AND THE LAW

BY

ERWIN I. J. ROSENTHAL

VIII

The Talmudic Background

GOD made man to serve Him by joyful obedience to His will. This will has been made known through Revelation which, for the Jew, took the form of Torah. It is this divinely revealed Torah which gives the Hebrew tribes their characteristic constitution.

The tribes, tradition tells us, accepted this constitution in the form of a covenant freely negotiated and freely entered into with God. Thus they became the people of Israel, the Jewish nation. The Jews as a nation have always considered the revelation at Sinai as the beginning of their history. They have never lost sight of that vital event. Their memory of it explains their unique historic consciousness and their continuity through and beyond such important moments of history as the Babylonian Exile, the end of the Jewish State in the war against Rome, the Crusades, and the expulsion from Spain in 1492. The divisions which criticism applies to the Jewish people into Pre-exilic and Post-exilic religion, into Biblical and Post-biblical Judaism, are for a Jew only so many stages of a continuous growth and development. And Mediæval Judaism, with which we are concerned in this lecture, is, in substance at least, the Judaism of the majority of Jews to-day. Any differences are due to those flexible adaptations and

modifications which characterize the history of the
Jewish people and explain the freshness and actuality
of the Jewish religion throughout the ages.

The rules of Jewish life are laid down in the Talmud.
The Talmud is based on the Mishnah, which in its
turn has its source in the Divine Torah, which it not
only explains but expands to supply the Jew with
a sure, reliable and valid guide for his entire life from
birth to death and in the hereafter.

Moses, Jewish tradition holds, not only received on
Sinai the Written Torah but also its interpretation in
the form of Oral Torah.[1]   The Sinaitic origin of the
entire Torah, both written and oral, may for the
jurist and the Bible critic be a fiction, but it certainly
was an unquestionable truth and reality for the
Jewish people.   With the help of rules of interpretation the Rabbis not only expounded the Torah to the
people but attempted successfully to relate all life to
it.   They were faced with the task of bringing this
changing world within the circumference of Torah.
They had to make the Torah answer all needs and
resolve all doubts.

The first stage in this process is the Mishnah
(*ca.* 200 C.E.).   But the foremost teachers of Judaism
found the Mishnah for practical purposes as inadequate without a fresh interpretation as their predecessors had found the written Torah.   They therefore
adapted and modified the Mishnah.   And the result
of about three centuries of such adaptation and
modification is the Talmud (*ca.* 500).

The end of the Jewish State in the year 70 C.E.

---

[1] Dr. Herford has dealt with the growth and meaning of this
Oral Torah, *above*, pp. 101 ff.   See also his *Talmud and Apocrypha*,
book ii.

released new forces which regenerated Judaism and
kept scattered Jewry together. But a heavy price had
to be paid for this feat of courage and determination :
the Jews had to be kept apart from the other nations
by numerous restrictions. That the Jews survived so
many political changes in various parts of the world
is due in the first place to the uncompromising
attitude of the generations of teachers in the time
between the codification of the Mishnah and of the
Talmud, and especially afterwards in much less
favourable conditions to the fundamental beliefs and
ideas of Judaism. This attitude was happily coupled
with a wise readiness to compromise in the less vital
sphere of inter-human relations in the interests of
peace and goodwill (*mipp'nē darchē shalōm*). The
Rabbis, aptly called the wise, realized at an early
stage in the Talmudic period that man has duties to
Cæsar as well as to God. They ruled that *the law of
the government is Law* (*dīna d'malchūta dīna*)—that is to
say, in matters of civil law the law of the state wherein
the Jews lived has precedence over Jewish civil law.
In practice this applied mainly to litigation between
Jews and non-Jews. But they always urged and, if
possible, insisted that inter-Jewish strife and dispute
be settled before a Jewish court. Thereby they helped
an autonomous Jewish cultural life to function
smoothly within the state.

As the Talmud throughout the Middle Ages (and
still in our own days) was the sure guide to which the
responsible leaders turned for their decisions, we must
enumerate very briefly a few of the principles which
the Talmudic teachers laid down in order to co-
ordinate life and law within the circumference of the
Divine Torah.

Profound changes not only in the material sphere but also in moral outlook had taken place since the interpretation of the written Torah was found necessary. It was essential, therefore, that the written word should be readjusted to meet the new circumstances if God's will was to rule supreme. The Rabbis knew that the letter killeth. They therefore tried to keep the spirit alive by giving the unalterable word a new meaning. They did this not to save the letter but to lead man to God by teaching him to live according to the spirit of the commandments.

The Talmud states the authority of the Rabbis. They are the legitimate heirs of the prophets of the Old Testament. *Prophecy was taken away from the prophets and given to the wise, and it has not been taken away from these (b. B. Bathra,* 12^b).[1] This heritage invested the Great *Beth Din* (Supreme Court) with authority to modify and often virtually set aside the written Torah. But no other court had this power, and no other court could annul a decision of the Great *Beth Din* unless it excelled it in wisdom and numbers. This principle, which was universally recognized from the very beginning, provided a sufficient safeguard against arbitrariness and ensured universal respect for the decisions of the Great *Beth Din* which were incorporated in the Talmud.

By modifications of the written Torah the Rabbis intended, in the first place, to raise the moral standard of the people, to humanize original harshness and to protect the weak. Thus no ordinance could be

[1] I am following here Dr. Herford, *loc. cit.*, as I consider his treatment the best and most valuable précis in English. The reader will find in chapter vi, " The Ethical Teaching on the Rabbinical Line," ample illustration of the problem under discussion.

enforced unless it was bearable by the majority
(*b. B. Bathra*, 60ᵇ). The Rabbis were fully aware of
the changes which had taken place in the intervening
centuries, and realized that new conditions created
new needs which were not met in the written Torah.
They therefore ruled that *the needs of the times* and *the
adjustment of human relations* justified a modification and
called for new regulations and rules not only to
maintain but also to raise the ethical standard.[1] But
not everything could be defined precisely, e.g. " the
weightier matters of the Law." These commandments
were *committed to the heart*. And even where minute
regulations by way of a *halachah* were fixed, they
constituted only the bare minimum. So much for
the Talmudic background.

The Period of the Geonim (589–1040)

That Jewry, scattered over the Islamic empire in
East and West and over Western Christian Europe,
did not disintegrate is due exclusively to the reign of
the Talmud. But the Talmud needed to be interpreted
and expanded. In the period between 589 and 1040
the Geonim determined the course of Jewish life.
They were the acknowledged teachers and leaders of
Jewry. Their influence was not confined to Babylonia,
where they presided over the academies. From all
over the world Jews journeyed to the Babylonian
seats of learning to listen to the interpretations of the
Talmud given by the Geonim. There they learnt to
apply Talmudic findings to present-day problems of
Jewish life, and returned to their homes equipped with
useful practical knowledge which they used for the

[1] See also Loewe, vol. i, especially pp. 144 ff.

benefit of their communities. Thus the Geonim made
the Talmud and its teaching accessible to Jewry at
large.

Quite naturally the juridical authority of the
Geonim was recognized throughout the Caliphate.
But why did the Jews in other parts of the world, who
were not subject to the Caliph in Baghdad, submit to
the authority of the Geonim ? What was this authority
and whence did it derive its power ?

In the Jewish theocracy where God was the ruler,
the King of kings, authority rested exclusively with
those who interpreted His will which was set forth in
the Torah. This authority belonged to men whose
knowledge and learning made them competent to
interpret the Torah, to guide the people in its ways
and to decide its application to everyday life. In
addition, ordination by an individual or a body of
authoritative teachers formally endorsed the worth of
such a teacher and entitled him to act as judge in
matrimonial cases, and in civil cases also in so far as
these were covered by the autonomy granted to the
respective Jewries, regional as well as local. Ordination in the full sense is possible in Palestine only, but
we find the practice among the German Rabbis of
the later Middle Ages—to quote one example—to
authorize their disciples to decide legal matters. In
this way only could Jewish life be maintained on the
traditional lines and legal authority kept alive in an
unbroken chain of successive teachers.

The Geonim themselves claimed to be the rightful
heirs and successors of the presidents of the Palestinian
Sanhedrin *ex officio*, and consequently demanded un-
conditional obedience to their enactments and decisions. They based these decisions on the Talmud

as a rule. By authoritative exposition of the Talmud they secured the continuity of Jewish life in its entirety and arrived at new rules to meet the fresh demands of changed circumstances. But occasionally they were obliged to depart from the Talmud, and actually declared that there was neither norm nor tradition for such departures.[1]

Thus they introduced an oath to be sworn by a debtor to the effect that he could not pay his creditor.[2] On the other hand they were so conscious of their inferiority to the Talmudic Rabbis that they dared not loosen a vow, feeling that this was beyond their power and right.[3] At the same time we find that they are less rigorous in court ceremonial, the reason being that they had no power to enforce the law in all its rigidity.[4]

Their regulations mostly took the form of an answer to a question addressed to them, often from another continent, and these *Responsa* (like the *Fatwās* of the Muslim jurists [5]) enjoyed binding legal force at any rate within the Geonic period. Towards the close of the Geonic period, and especially from the eleventh century onward, the codifiers of Jewish law subjected the Geonic findings to a close scrutiny and did not

[1] The following account is mainly based on H. Tykocinski's critical monograph, *Die Gaonäischen Verordnungen* (Berlin, 1929), to which the reader is referred for a more detailed study of the subject.   [2] *Ibid.*, p. 67.

[3] The later Talmudic Rabbis adopted the same attitude to the earlier teachers : see the present writer's *Islam*, vol. ii of this series, p. 173.

[4] Tykocinski, *loc. cit.*, p. 168, in the name of Maimonides, to whose labours we owe much of our knowledge about the legal activity of the Geonim.

[5] See Professor Gibb's lecture on *Law and Religion in Islam*, above, p. 162.

hesitate to rule them out if they were found to be
contrary to Talmudic decision. This applies particularly to Maimonides. But throughout the Geonic
period the Geonic findings ruled supreme.

The formulæ which they employed in their *Responsa*
throw additional light on their authority. If due
allowance be made for Rabbinic diction and mediæval
expressions of style, the exalted position of the Geonim
as the authoritative interpreters of the Divine Torah
and as links in an unbroken chain of Oral Tradition
stands out clear. Thus we find expressions like *Thus
has Heaven revealed unto us*, or *With Divine Help we have
found*. They conclude their decisions with *May God
grant us to decide according to the Torah and to teach
according to valid decision*. More frequently they phrase
their answers, especially to foreign correspondents,
thus : *May God reveal unto thee . . . and unto all the
scholars and disciples of the city, the Torah of wisdom and
of understanding. . . .*[1]

We may sum up briefly the significance of the
Geonim and the characteristic features of their
activity by saying that they tried to preserve the
essentials of Judaism intact, to impart to their generation the fundamental beliefs and ideas of the Jewish
religion, and to keep up the *morale* of the Jews in
family life as well as in social and commercial relations, in the spirit though not always in the letter of
Torah, and, wherever possible, in keeping with the
rulings of the Talmudic sages. Development there
undoubtedly is, even change, but never and nowhere a
defection from the divinely revealed truth or from an
interpretation compatible with established tradition.
It is a development within the confines of the Torah.

[1] See *Jew. Enc.*, xi, article *She'elot u-Teshubot*.

Their rulings were necessitated by the rapid changes which Jewish economic and social life was undergoing in the expanding Islamic empire.

One of the results of this expansion was a closer contact with the Muslim world. Apparently this contact had some detrimental effects. For we read [1] that the Geonim permitted that a letter of divorce be issued to an unmanageable wife at once instead of after twelve months as the Talmud enjoined. This measure would prevent Jewesses from applying to a non-Jewish, that is to say Muslim, court.

As the result of growing commerce and trade landed property decreased in favour of movable possessions. It is only to be expected that safeguards had to be found : (a) to preserve agricultural estates in Jewish hands, and (b) to protect debtors and creditors alike, especially in the matter of liability in case of death, and consequently to protect the heirs.[2] To effect this special oaths and penalty by ban were introduced. In this connexion the following case is noteworthy : One of the Geonim had to decide whether a ban pronounced by a local Jewish court by order of the king was valid or not. The king, by this ban, forbade that the property of a deceased person, which he wished to confiscate, should be handed over to the rightful heirs. The Gaon decided that such a ban, pronounced under threat of illegal force, was invalid. For in this case *the law of the government was not law*, as the king had no legal right to his action.[3]

From what we have said before on the genesis and development of Jewish law it is evident that the

---

[1] Tykocinski, *loc. cit.*, pp. 15 ff.
[2] *Ibid.*, pp. 52 ff., with a lucid comment by Maimonides.
[3] Tykocinski, *loc. cit.*, p. 132.

regulations and particularly the *Responsa* of the Geonim covered the whole range of human activity and thought. The Jewish Torah has always been all-comprehensive.

Religious ceremonies are naturally among the subjects dealt with. Here we find the Geonim, as the Rabbis before and after them, very reluctant to endorse the practice of ceremonies which spring from customs foreign to Judaism. In most cases these were borrowed from the outside world as the result of friendly contact with neighbours. The same applies to habits of everyday life and to deep-rooted customs of an almost legal character.[1] But they permitted such practices locally because they were so deeply entrenched and so common that no authoritative veto could have prevailed against them.

Custom (*minhag*) is undoubtedly a principal source of law from its early stages throughout the history of Jewish law, but, as in Islam, it was always acknowledged as second in rank to the revealed law. Many a custom was legalized because it formed an inseparable part of the national life and expressed the ideas and beliefs of the people. In times prior to the close of the Talmud, it appears that many a custom was embodied in oral Torah as a halachah of (alleged) Mosaic-Sinaitic origin.[2] In later times the Rabbis of each generation tried to adapt such popular customs to Jewish ethical conceptions and to bring them into line with religious ideas peculiar to Judaism. They made modifications and slight changes in their performance, and they adduced reasons which

[1] Cf. Gibb, *above*, pp. 159 ff., on ʿāda and inṣāf.

[2] Cf. the present writer's *Islam*, vol. ii, p. 169, and Rabinowitz, *ibid.*, p. 206 to end of paper.

made such ceremonics and customs appear as Jewish and of great antiquity and as symbols of a Jewish idea or belief. They sought only to suppress their superstitious origin and character.[1] But they did not always succeed, and, at times, had to overlook their existence and thus make them innocuous. Customs differed considerably according to the land of origin and practice. But the Rabbis took every precaution to see that any doubtful practices did not undermine the fundamental conceptions of pure, ethical Jewish monotheism.

So far we have spoken only of the Jews under Muslim rule. Apart from Babylonia, there were large communities in Egypt, North Africa, Yemen and the European possessions of Islam, chiefly in Spain. All these were under Geonic influence much longer than the communities in France and Germany. But with the end of the Caliphate of Baghdad in 1040 the Geonim disappeared.

The Western Communities in the later Middle Ages

Western Jewry lived under the feudal Christian system, or, more correctly, the Jews were excluded from the Christian society. We are not concerned here with their legal status, but rather with the effects of their precarious economic position and social calling on the development of Jewish law in these realms.

A Jew could not hold a fief *qua* Jew. If a lord took

---

[1] Professor J. Z. Lauterbach has dealt with this important question in two exhaustive critical essays in the *Hebrew Union College Annual*: "The Ceremony of Breaking a Glass at Weddings" (ii, 1925), and "*Tashlik:* a Study in Jewish Ceremonies" (xi, 1937).

away land from the peasant owners they could at
least receive it back as fief. But this did not apply in
the case of the Jew. Thus, inevitably, he was driven
from the land, notwithstanding the strenuous efforts
of the Rabbis to keep landed property in Jewish hands
and thus prevent the Jews from entering commerce and
trade, and in the later Middle Ages money-lending,
which were the only possibilities left to them as means
of livelihood. For the Jews were barred from the
guilds and consequently from the crafts. Regulations
and ordinances (*taqqanoth*) passed by synods of several
communities, notably by those along the Rhine with
seats of learning ever growing in importance and soon
to provide the West with teachers, included measures
to save Jewish landed estates by exempting them from
communal taxes.[1] But without avail !

The growing Jewish participation in export and
import trade called for measures by the local Jewish
courts. Inter-continental travel was risky because of
perils by road and by sea. Not only had safe-conduct
to be secured from the territorial princes and muni-
cipalities, but also the families remaining behind had
to be provided for. Most important of all, considerable capital was needed. Now, the taking of interest
from a fellow-Jew was forbidden by Biblical law. But
without credit the bare existence of a large number of
Jewish families was threatened.

How could this difficulty be overcome without going
against the law ? The answer is : by the institution
of sleeping partnerships. To prevent such partnerships from being nothing but disguised lending on

[1] The whole body of these ordinances is dealt with in
L. Finkelstein's *Jewish Self-Government in the Middle Ages* (New
York, 1924), where full information is available. See p. 12 f.

interest, the synods of the early thirteenth century enforced a decision which had binding legal character. It permitted such financial transactions only if the sleeping partner (or creditor) shared in losses as well as in profits.[1]

This, which is only one example of a large number of emergency measures to meet particular needs of the moment, is strictly in accordance with the Talmudical principle and practice [2] of adapting Jewish life and law to changing and changed conditions. In modern times, such regulations form part of commercial law, and it seems strange to us that they have any relation to Revelation and revealed law. But from the standpoint of an all-comprehensive religious " Law," however, it is quite natural that economic life should be regulated in agreement with the spirit of Torah. He whose business practice flatly contradicted the Torah and its injunctions incurred formidable punishment for his transgression in the form of an oath or ban. But as there was always—on religious grounds—a good deal of reluctance to let a Jew swear an oath, the purpose was in many cases achieved by a curse. Most frequently, however, the law was enforced by a penalty which, next to the taking of life itself, was the severest penalty of all : by the ban (herem).

Finkelstein deals at length with the various forms of ban and I cannot go into detail here.[3] They all

---

[1] L. Finkelstein, *Jewish Self-Government in the Middle Ages*, p. 59.

[2] See *above*, p. 173.

[3] It is not always possible to trace the source of a particular ban. Some scholars are of opinion that the herem hay-yishub to forbid settlement without the consent of the community, e.g., owes its existence to the guild system with its restriction of free

have in common social ostracism and exclusion from the religious life of the community. The house of worship and communal meeting was closed to a person under *herem* ; he was unfit to perform any religious ceremony : he was, in a word, excommunicated. The threat of this formidable weapon as a rule sufficed to enforce synodal or communal decisions, and the result was a strengthening of Rabbinic authority and the maintenance of community life in peace and order. The ban might easily be misused for personal ends, and the responsible leaders tried to limit the use of it. But this was not always possible, and taking into ban gradually became too frequent to serve its legitimate purpose.

Provided the Jews paid taxes and tributes in exchange for the right to live, the state or municipality did not interfere with the life and affairs of the community. Consequently they did not lend their secular arm to enforce the ordinances of the Rabbis. How, then, did the courts enjoy authority sufficient to enforce their decisions unopposed ?

The constitution of a court in conformity with Rabbinic requirements was the sign of a properly organized community. In its turn the community recognized the court and abided by its decisions.

settlement and practice of a craft. This right was conditional upon the consent of the particular guild. Dr. Rabinowitz, in a study on this ban in *Jew. Quart. Rev.* (1938, pp. 217 ff.), adduces convincing evidence for the Talmudic origin of it. I venture to suggest that both views combined lead to a more satisfactory explanation. The guild system made it necessary for the Jews to introduce the measure precisely in the form in which it there existed. But it had to be justified in Jewish law and, if possible, a Talmudic precedent or analogy had to be found. Therefore, the *taqqanah* was theoretically based upon the Talmud, as Rabinowitz shows.

Thus there was established a reciprocity between the community organized as a legal body and the court having judicial and administrative functions. The basis of the authority of the courts was not strong enough without a link with the past. This link was supplied by the claim of the Rabbis that they inherited their authority through their learning in tradition. Although some German Rabbis differed in their views as to who were the rightful heirs of the ancient *Sanhedrin* (Supreme Court), whether the local courts or the greatest scholars of any generation,[1] they were unanimous in holding that juridical authority was derived from the undisputed authority of the Sanhedrin of old, and was therefore legitimate authority. In practice, it was clear that a regulation must be pronounced by the recognized scholars of the generation before it could be recognized as legally binding by all or by a majority of communities. As in the days of the Sanhedrin, the majority (in any community or of a number of communities) decided, and the minority had to abide loyally by the decision. Thus was achieved that consensus which was a prerequisite of legality, just as *ijma'* in Islam.[2]

Measures affecting a community could not run counter to public opinion and, as has been stated above (p. 175) as an important Talmudic principle, could only be enforced with the approval of the majority, which must be in a position to carry it out.

Disputes within a community were, again in accordance with Talmudic principle, decided by the eminent teachers of a neighbouring community.

[1] See Finkelstein, *loc. cit.*, pp. 50 ff.
[2] See Gibb, *above*, pp. 157 ff., and the present writer's *Islam*, vol. ii, p. 172.

Passing reference must be made at least to the large number of regulations and ordinances in matters of marriage and divorce. It is a curious fact that monogamy, though practised for centuries in Jewish communities in Europe at least, was legalized only about the year 1000 by Rabbenu Gershom, to whom we also owe the prohibition of plural marriage and the enactment of compulsory divorce of a bigamist.[1] The question of plural marriage was of practical importance in connexion with the Levirate marriage (*Yibbum*) and the Biblical rules governing it.[2] These injunctions are classical examples of regard for human feelings based on a higher ethical standard. Originally a stigma was attached to the refusal of *Yibbum*, and the ceremony of *Ḥaliṣah* was considered dishonourable and humiliating. But now it was considered meritorious and encouraged, even enforced.[3] The rights of the wife were now more respected, and as a rule a husband could no longer divorce his wife against her will or, rather, without her consent.[4] A wife was also protected against ill-treatment by her husband, and a man who left his wife to go to a seat of learning to study Torah and Talmud was obliged to return within a definite but not too long period.[5] The examples we have just given may suffice to show the tendency of mediæval legal activity to stress the ethical side of the Torah and to reinterpret and apply ancient customs on a higher moral plane.

[1] Finkelstein, *loc. cit.*, pp. 23 ff. See also Rabinowitz, vol. ii, pp. 207 f.

[2] Deut. xxv. 5–10 ; cf. also Ruth iv. 10.

[3] Finkelstein, *loc. cit.*, p. 27.

[4] *Ibid.*, pp. 29 f.

[5] *Ibid.*, p. 44.

The so-called Law Codes [1]

This tendency is amply attested by the several codes which were compiled from the ninth century onwards. Their object was not to stifle the progressive development of Jewish law, but rather to supply a handbook for the use of the teacher who acted as judge by collecting and sifting the accumulated material which tended to confuse rather than to guide the judges. The mere fact that the Precepts (*miṣwoth*), both positive and negative, comprise all spheres of human life in its relation to God and one's neighbour [2] excludes from the start the coming into being of a Law Code in our sense of the word.

In the Middle Ages these codes alone made possible a normal inter-community life by summing up the norm out of a mass of single cases and decisions. Moreover, the difficult political and, consequently, economic position of Jewry made regional and local adjustments continually necessary and thus endangered and obscured the norm based on the Talmud. The codes clarified and rectified life in all its aspects, and served not only as the basis for legal practice but also for further and higher development.

A description of this whole literature in detail is not relevant to our discussion in this series. We limit ourselves to an outline of the work of Maimonides : the monumental structure of the *Mishneh Torah*, preceded by his Commentary on the Mishnah and his

[1] See, for a full description, *Jew. Enc.*, vii, article " Law, Codification of."

[2] The division of all commandments into these two groups is already Talmudical and was adopted by the mediæval Jewish thinkers as traditional.

Sefer ham-Miṣwoth, the first really scientific exposition of the 613 Biblical commandments.

Without the previous labours of generations of Rabbis who had tried to bring order and system into the accumulated material, his own work would have been unthinkable, even impossible. And yet without his scientific method which enabled him to present the complete Torah in one great system, subdivided into fourteen books, it is difficult to see how Jewish life could have endured. The *Mishneh Torah* has set the standard for subsequent centuries and forms the principal basis of the still valid Code of Josef Caro (the *Shulḥan 'Arūch*). It has profoundly influenced its followers no less than its opponents.

In form it is perhaps the finest example of the synthesis of Greek philosophy, in its Aristotelian perfection of systematic clear thinking and method, with the traditional interpretation of the written Torah which had evolved its own particular method in the course of centuries. The diction is perfect, the style simple, the language pure Hebrew. The unwieldy mass of Halachah is reduced to bare essentials.

The minutest detail receives significance because it is conceived as an indispensable member of a system which gives a complete answer to the problem of the end of man. The commandments are to be performed in order to prepare man for the perception of God as perfectly as is humanly possible. The knowledge of *Existing Things* fills the faithful adherent of Torah with admiration for God's Wisdom as manifested in the world of His creation, and with awe of God's Might ; it leads man to the service of God's Will in love. Conscious service proceeding from love and for the sake of love ensures that ultimate spiritual happiness of which the philosophers speak but which only the perfect Torah and its fulfilment can guarantee.

We cannot here treat of the many aspects of Maimonides' Code, nor of the criteria which Maimonides applied as the test of valid Halachah. But we must at least sum up briefly the contribution which Maimonides as a creative halachist has made to Jewish law, from the point of view of legal development and ethical advance within the perfect Torah divinely revealed.

Needless to say, for him as for any responsible teacher before and after him, the Talmud formed the natural basis and centre of Jewish life and law. He claimed, quite in keeping with tradition, for himself and his generation the same right, which he considered a duty, of reinterpreting the Talmud in the language and for the needs of his time, which he allowed to every generation from the earliest days of Israel's history. He saw that each generation made laws and regulations and followed customs to meet the requirements of the moment in matters of Forbidden and Permitted, Binding and Voluntary.[1]

[1] Introduction to *Mishneh Torah* (edit. Amsterdam, 1701). This introduction and that to *Seder Z^{e}ra'im*, in his Commentary to the Mishnah, briefly recount the history of the Halachah from the standpoint of Jewish tradition, with a definition of its principles and a classification of the laws. See the papers in *Moses ben Maimon* (Leipzig, 1908), and in *Moses Maimonides* (London, 1935), dealing with Maimonides as a halachist. Ch. Tschernowitz's *Toledoth ha-halakah* (New York, 1934) contains, in the introduction, a full discussion of Maimonides' attitude to the Torah. So far two parts have appeared : Part I, dealing, apart from the introduction, with the development of Law in the Biblical age ; Part II, " The First Commonwealth to the time of Ezra " (1936), with such topics as kingship, priesthood, etc. Useful comparisons with Greek and Roman laws and institutions enhance the value of the important book.

The principle that *the Torah speaks in the language of
man* accounts for the necessary limitation of the
miṣwoth. They were propounded in the language
which the particular generation could understand,
and were destined to administer to their needs. As
the Torah is given by God in His wisdom and mercy
to Israel for all times, the *miṣwoth* are eternally
binding upon those who are under the Torah. If they
are to retain their authority and validity they must
be reinterpreted as occasion demands. Moreover,
the *miṣwoth* were the unalterable basis for new regulations which were derived from them by analogy or
other rules of interpretation.[1]

Maimonides saw that his task was to supply his
generation with such an interpretation in order to
help his fellows to attain their highest end. He stated
his interpretation in the language of his day, that is
to say of Greek philosophy (physics and metaphysics)
as transmitted through the *Falāsifa*, the Muslim
philosophers. In doing so he knew himself to stand
loyally and faithfully on the ground of the Torah.
He could never have erected his system without an
extensive knowledge of the laws of physics, mathematics, astronomy, agriculture, and the like. The
Talmud gives ample proof that the Rabbis of the
Mishnaic-Talmudic age possessed such knowledge,
without which they could not have fixed the Halachah.
We need think only of the Calendar. But Maimonides
went a step further by frankly stating that the
knowledge of these Rabbis—time-bound as it necessarily was—was not perfect, but often inadequate and
faulty. He claimed only the right to supply, if he
were able, a better, more scientific explanation,

[1] See the present writer's *Islam*, vol. ii, pp. 173 ff.

compatible with the results of Greek science and philosophy.

This is reflected in his method, which was quite new, of prefacing the orders of the Talmud with introductions of a general character in which he set out methodically the principles underlying the regulation, its significance within the system. By this method he hoped to make clear that the purpose of all commandments is to lead man to his perfection by serving God, both in action and in thought. He attached, therefore, special importance to the theoretical commandments, in particular that of perception and knowledge of God, in so far as through them man obtained sound ideas and was drawn near to the true conception of *Existing Things* and their divine Creator. But he did not underrate the practical side of life. Again and again he stressed the essential unity of theory and practice. More than other men, the *Hacham*, the wise, the scholar, the thinker, must show forth this unity. Just as the wise man is recognized by his wisdom and thoughts which distinguish him from others, so he must be recognizable by his actions.[1] These actions are prescribed in the Torah, which is the emanation of God's absolute wisdom.

The identification of Torah with Wisdom is as old as the Hebrew Wisdom literature. The Maccabean age incorporated certain Greek ideas and customs. These did not hellenize Judaism, but rather created a developed Judaism which held successfully its ground against Hellenism. In the same way mediæval Judaism was able to " modernize " Judaism (if one could use such a word), to bring out its inherent truth with the help of Greek science and philosophy. This

[1] See *Mishneh Torah, Hilchoth De'oth*, iii. 2 and v. 1.

explains why Maimonides introduced his code with the *Sefer ham-Maddaʿ*, in which he postulated knowledge of the physical order and of God as the Creator of the world *ex nihilo*, and in which he propounded the essential beliefs and fundamental principles of Judaism (among them Monotheism, Free Will, Reward and Punishment, Repentance and Forgiveness, the Messiah), as ideas of the Torah and as component indispensable factors of the true faith in God whom to know is the primary object of religion. Indeed, this philosophical superstructure explains the true significance and purpose of the Torah. It relates every minute detail of the Halachah, expounded in the code, to this great purpose by laying out the principles on which Judaism rests. The application of these principles and their realization in a God-centred life are the function of the Halachah.

Abraham, the beloved of God, is the personification of the ideal after which every man should strive. He who serves out of love studies the Torah and keeps the *miṣwoth* ; he who walks in the paths of wisdom not to reap worldly gain or out of fear of Evil or to inherit the Good, but in order to do what is true because it is true. Such a one realizes the ideal love. And this is the meaning of the commandment *And thou shalt love the Lord thy God*. When a man loves God with the right love he does all the *miṣwoth* out of love.[1] This love is based on knowledge and differs according to the individual capacity for knowledge. The sciences help man to know his Maker. But there are things man cannot understand with his human intellect. They can be understood only by prophecy and foresight. For God's knowledge is different from man's

---

[1] *Mishneh Torah, Hilchoth Tᵉshubah*, x. 2 ; see also x. 3.

knowledge ; therefore man can never discover the nature of the Creator.[1] But through his experience of God's miracles and His boundless wisdom man passionately desires to know God.[2] This knowledge leads to love and fear of God.

On the basis of his ethical conception Maimonides, whilst admitting the usual distinction between man's duties towards his fellow and man's duties towards God, completely subordinates the former to the latter. For every commandment which aims at moral betterment, right conduct or sound knowledge and understanding falls under the category of duties of man to God.

But Maimonides was not content merely to lay down the rule of right conduct. He wished to find the reason underlying the precepts, if the reason lay within the reach of the human intellect. Trained in rational thinking through his study of philosophy, and at the same time convinced of the infallible wisdom and truth of the divinely revealed Torah, he could not admit that the Torah contained anything which ran counter to reason. He is thus sometimes forced to adopt an allegorical, figurative meaning of Scripture. Where the plain, literal meaning did not satisfy him he looked for and found an inner, hidden meaning. With this question we cannot deal here. But the result of this method was that in a number of cases where actual commandments are concerned he discovered a reason for such commandments which was contrary to tradition. Those among his contemporaries and successors who held with some ancient Rabbis that man is not to investigate into the reasons of the commandments, naturally attacked his rational

[1] *Ib., loc. cit.*, v. 5.   [2] *Ib., Hilchoth Yᵉsōḏē Hat-Torah*, ii.

explanation.[1] And yet he believed as firmly and
passionately as any naïve, unquestioning believer in
the perfect wisdom of the Divine Torah in its written
as well as in its oral form, and never questioned their
indivisibility as revelation of the eternal truth.

His code was attacked for yet another reason.
Contrary to his precursors, Maimonides did not give
his reasons for his decisions nor did he cite his sources.
There can be no doubt that Maimonides' method
might eventually have led to a result which he
certainly did not intend. The finality of his decision
might some day rule out free discussion, and with
it development.[2] But he adopted this method for
practical purposes and not through lack of reverence.
His reverence for the Talmud and for the Geonim,
despite the criticism he often levels against them, was
equal to that of any of his contemporaries.

A case in point is his treatment of the Liturgy.
Here, he accepts as established only what is Talmudic;
everything else he either omits, refutes, or at its best
tolerates as *minhag*.[3] Such reverence was based on the
conviction that the Pharisees sat on the throne of
Moses and that the Talmudic sages were the heirs of
the prophets.[4]

That Maimonides makes the Talmudic opinion his
own shows better than anything else the continuity of

[1] E.g. his reasons for the sacrifices.

[2] He did, however, not wish to supersede with his code the
Talmud as far as study was concerned. But he claimed to have
settled the Halachah for all practical purposes. If he thus
claimed an authority which no individual Rabbi ever did, he
did it in order to end confusion and to lay down a sure guide for
all who had to apply the Halachah to everyday life.

[3] See Elbogen, " Der Ritus im Mishne Thora," in *Moses ben
Maimon* (Leipzig, 1908).

[4] See *above*, p. 174.

Jewish history of which we spoke in the beginning of this lecture. It further shows that such a critical mind did not hesitate to acknowledge the continuity of prophetic tradition.

In true prophetic tradition all Rabbis of all periods of Jewish history insisted upon faith, knowledge and ethics no less than on ceremonial. All commandments are of equal importance as part of the one indivisible Revelation. We are therefore not surprised to find among the *taqqanoth* of the mediæval Rabbis the injunction that everybody should set aside a definite time for study,[1] alongside with regulations concerning family life and right conduct in commercial matters.

We have dwelt at such length upon the problem of Jewish life and law in the Middle Ages because it illustrates how divinely revealed Torah can be kept alive and be ultimately authoritative in such a way that it answers to all the requirements of a life led under entirely different conditions, material, social and spiritual, without sacrificing the least of its essentials. This was possible only through the living tradition handed down unbroken and unquestioned from generation to generation of teachers who did not lose sight of human life with all its changes but at the same time kept their unwavering faith in the eternally true Divine Revelation. Everything was of equal importance. The Torah was an indivisible whole. As a *fountain of living waters* this Torah was a reality and an ever fresh personal experience for all those who lived under it.

[1] Already in *Pirkē Aḇoth*, i. 15.

The Philosophers and Divine Revelation

The treatment of our problem is, however, not exhausted with the survey of the development of the Halachah within Judaism itself. The progress of revelation—that is, the progressive interpretation of the original, perfect Torah—was challenged by the ever-growing authority of Aristotle in the field of the philosophy of the natural sciences, which provided the human mind with an answer to the questions relating to man's place in the universe, his destiny and his purpose.

Aristotle, like Plato, was brought to the Jews through the Falasifa. Because Judaism and Islam were essentially alike, Aristotle was harmonized by both as much as possible with revelation. In other words, a speculative system devised by mortal man was subjected to the test of the Divine will as revealed in a Torah. Unless we realize from the very beginning this fundamental relation which is the natural outcome of the universally accepted superiority of Revelation, we shall fail to perceive that mediæval man did not admit that faith and reason are mutually exclusive. Where we moderns allege an unbridgeable and elemental gulf, the thinkers of the Middle Ages saw that the Divine purpose and human thought were at one.

As is clear from the brief sketch given above, Maimonides' philosophical treatment of the Halachah has not only saved its life but has also acted as a wholesome stimulant of further development. And it is the Halachah and not philosophic speculation which has determined the future course of Judaism. Unfortunately we cannot here develop historically the test to

which speculation subjected revelation—not to undermine and question its authority but to explain it in
the language of a generation given to philosophic
thought !—from Sa'adya to Don Isaac Abravanel.
Also, I am—much to my regret—obliged to forgo
the proof of what follows and to reserve it for another
occasion.[1]

It is obvious that Maimonides was indebted to
previous generations of halachists for his own halachic
work, just as his philosophic work was built up on the
attempts of philosophers who preceded him. But
because he far surpassed earlier treatises by his
synthesis of Hebraic and Greek thought in his *Morē
N'buchim* and by his perfect mastery of Aristotelian
philosophy, as perfect as possible in his day, we may
confine ourselves to Maimonides and leave aside his
predecessors. Another reason for our choice of
Maimonides is that his *Morē* was the basis of the
works of later Jewish thinkers, though they differed
from it either by their greater emphasis on the Torah
(Crescas, Albo, Abravanel) or of Aristotle (Gersonides).
The reasons for this development are to be found in
the better knowledge of Aristotle through Averroes'
Commentaries on the one hand and in the general
tendency of the times away from speculation on the
other. To these causes must be added, in the case of
Judaism, the considerable deterioration of the political,
social and economic situation brought about by the
hostility of the Church and by the nascent nationalism
which increased their vigilance against possible danger
from within. One more reason for our choice of

---

[1] A detailed study of the conception of Torah and law in
mediæval Jewish philosophy by way of an historical survey from
Sa'adya to Abravanel will, I hope, soon be published.

Maimonides is that he influenced the Scholastics [1] and Hugo Grotius.[2]

We consider here only the fundamental question of the relative aims and merits of Divine and human law. As the wider problem of Revelation and Reason took this form in the Middle Ages, such a discussion will at the same time attempt an answer to the problem as a whole.

The premises which guided the thinkers on this matter may be summed up as follows :

(i) Not one of them—not even Gersonides who went furthest with Aristotle—ever doubted the Divine origin and wisdom of the Torah.

(ii) They were all convinced of the ultimate inadequacy of human reason ever to perceive the true essence of God or to understand fully everything God had created.[3]

(iii) They held fast to there being only *one* truth, that of Torah, and they held that philosophy taught the same truth, but in a way different from and in the last resort inferior to that of Torah, much as human reason is inferior to Divine wisdom. But at the same time some of them held that philosophy, being the highest achievement of human intellect, can best explain what is within man's competence.

(iv) Only prophecy reveals the truth which is taught in different measure by the Torah and

---

[1] See Jakob Guttmann : *Die Scholastik d. 13. Jahrhunderts in ihren Beziehungen zum Judentum u. z. jüdischen Literatur* (Breslau, 1902), especially pp. 85–120 ; and *Das Verhältnis des Thomas von Aquino z. Judentum u. z. jüd. Literatur* (Göttingen, 1891), especially pp. 31–92, concerning Maimonides.

[2] See Professor I. Husik, " Natural Law, Hugo Grotius and the Bible," in *Hebrew Union College Annual*, 1925.

[3] See Maimonides' *Morē*, I, ch. 31, and *Eight Chapters*, ed. Gorfinkle (Hebrew text), ch. viii, p. 53, line 15 ff.

philosophy. Consequently only prophetic " law " and not the Greek *Nomos* of Plato can lead man to his ultimate perfection and happiness. At the same time it must be stressed that acquaintance with Plato's *Republic* and *Laws* led Maimonides in particular to a deeper understanding of the Torah as the ideal constitution for Israel, and made him stress the political character of that Torah.

(v) Lastly it should be remembered (*a*) that all these thinkers accepted oral Torah as binding as the written and insisted on their indivisibility, and (*b*) that, whatever they said or did, they said or did under and not outside or against the whole Torah.

They used their reason, God's most gracious and essential gift to man, in order to find out the meaning of the Torah and its *miṣwoth*. In so doing they practised an intelligent reasonable faith as opposed to a naïve, blind one. They likewise used their reason to scrutinize the Halachah. They accepted it as binding, but at times differed from the Talmudic teachers in the motives which they assigned for a certain decision or injunction.[1]

Divine and Human " Law "

Broadly speaking, all philosophers prior to Maimonides distinguish within the Torah precepts of reason and precepts of revelation.[2] They held that

---

[1] In connexion with this whole question it is significant that the Aristotelian Gersonides as well as the most important opponent of Aristotle, Crescas, intended to outdistance Maimonides, not only in the field of philosophy by challenging his *Morē*, but even in the field of Halachah. But both died before they had written codes against the *Mishneh Torah*.

[2] I cannot deal here with all the varieties and shades but must refer to the fuller treatment, see n. 1, p. 197.

human reason would have arrived through experience at the first group even without the help of revelation, because precepts like *Thou shalt not kill, steal, commit adultery* are absolutely necessary and they are common to all nations.[1]

Reason does not postulate the second group. Wherefore its commandments cannot be understood rationally. They are the outcome of God's mercy and goodness and, if obeyed, increase man's happiness and ensure his perfection.

But though man would have arrived at the laws accessible to reason and demanded by it, unaided by revelation, he would have done so after a very long time, and only in general : he could not have fixed their particulars. Also, man's knowledge is imperfect and opinion among men is varied. These factors together make unanimity impossible and therefore make the enforcement of law equally impossible.

Maimonides held that the scholars who were of this opinion *suffered from the illness of Qalām*.[2] His own idea

---

[1] See Husik, *loc. cit.*, for a full treatment of Natural Law in Roman Law, Augustine, Thomas Aquinas and Hugo Grotius with regard to the Old Testament. Cf. also Fr. McNabb, " St. Thomas Aquinas and Law " (*Blackfriars*, May 1929). That Judaism does not consider even the seven " Noachian Laws " as Natural Law but as divinely revealed external laws is shown by Professor I. Heinemann in a paper closely connected with Husik's and our problem under discussion, entitled " Die Lehre vom Ungeschriebenen Gesetz im Jüdischen Schrifttum," in *Hebrew Union College Annual*, iv, 1927. Though mainly concerned with Philo's *Nomos agraphos*, the author follows its history up through Rabbinic literature. For the seven Noachian Laws see *Jew. Enc.*, vii, and especially *Enc. Jud.*, vii, *s.v.* " Gesetze."

[2] Muslim scholasticism. Maimonides' criticism is directed against Saʿadya in the first place (*Eight Chapters*, vi. 36) ; cf. the whole chapter. He divides the laws into ceremonial and judicial (*Morē*, III, ch. 26). See also Fr. McNabb, *below*, p. 219, note.

of the Torah consists in a blend of the traditional view
of the divinely revealed, absolutely perfect and eternally binding *Torah* and the Platonic *Nomos* which
forms the constitution of the Ideal State and is laid
down by philosophers and enacted by the philosopher-
king.[1]

The Rabbis of Mishnah and Talmud saw that their
foremost task was to keep the Jews together as a
separate entity and as the world's witnesses to pure
ethical monotheism. To this purpose they prepared
the Jews morally and spiritually for the restoration to
their ancient political sovereignty in the land of Israel
in the Messianic future. If this political momentum
was implicitly present at their early day, it came
prominently to the fore in the Middle Ages under the
influence of Plato's political teaching as transmitted
through Alfārābī and his successors.[2]

[1] A. Menes, *Die vorexilischen Gesetze Israels* (Giessen, 1928),
draws a parallel between the constitution of ancient Israel and
of the Greek city-state. His attempt to explain the laws of the
Pentateuch through the economic and social conditions, especially in connexion with the transition from barter to money-
economy, should be noticed and pursued. He rightly emphasizes
further the democratic character of ancient Israel. The comparison with the Greek city-state should be closely investigated
in connexion with mediæval political thought.

[2] For a fuller treatment of Maimonides' thought the reader is
referred to the present writer's earlier study, "Maimonides'
Conception of State and Society" in *Moses Maimonides* (London,
1935), where Messianism is briefly dealt with as an integral part
of Maimonides' "political" philosophy. It seems to me now
that Plato rather helped to bring to fruition a conception of
Torah implicit in Judaism than that he actually influenced
Maimonides by giving him a new idea. Cf., especially,
Maimonides' elaborate treatment of all those laws which were
in his day of purely theoretical character as they applied only
to Palestine. Their inclusion into the code is intelligible only
under the Messianic aspect, and reflects the Messianic expectancy
of the time. The Greek conception of "political" ethics is in

The fusion of the two conceptions, the Hebraic and the Greek, resulted in the ideal ruler who is prophet, lawgiver and king in one person. Maimonides owes his acquaintance with Plato to Alfārābī, and his political view-point is due—in a literary connexion at least—to Abraham ibn Daud, whose 'Emunah Ramah is in many important points the true precursor of the Morē. Yehudah Hal-lewi already shows some familiarity with Plato's Republic. But Maimonides is the first to develop fully the idea of the Torah as the ideal and alone perfect constitution.[1] Albo only developed Maimonides' ideas.[2]

In Maimonides' conception, at the one end stands God who has made known His will through Moses the greatest of prophets and the ideal ruler ; at the other end is man as a citizen with definite' duties towards society and State. Man needs society for his existence. The State protects him and directs him to his ultimate perfection. This perfection consists in perceiving God by lovingly serving Him. It is possible only through the rule of law under a perfect leader.[3]

its totalitarian claim very much akin to the Jewish conception of Torah. But there is this decisive difference, that the former is the result of human aspiration, and the latter the gift of unerring Divine revelation inspired by absolute justice. One is almost tempted to express the distinction by calling it " political ethics " among the Greeks, but " ethical politics " among the Jews. See also on this point Fr. McNabb, " St. Thomas Aquinas and Law," p. 6 f. of the offprint. The present writer's " Politische Gedanken bei Ibn Bājja " in Monatsschrift f. d. Geschichte u. Wissenschaft d. Judentums (1937), pp. 153 ff., further compares Maimonides' thought with the Falasifa under the aspect of Torah and Nomos in the political sense.

[1] See, particularly, Morē, II, ch. 39, where the Divine Torah is contrasted with the human laws, like the laws of the Greeks, etc.

[2] In his 'Iqqarim (ed. I. Husik).

[3] See the present writer's " Maimonides' Conception," etc., loc. cit., pp. 197 ff., and the passages in the Morē quoted there.

There are various degrees of human perfection. The highest is the perfection of the intellect, which consists in the perception of *Existing Things* and of God Himself as much as is humanly possible. But contemplation as the highest aim in itself is ruled out, for the perception of God is only possible in active service of His will as laid down in the Torah, by imitating His ways and thus attaining His love.[1]

The superiority of Torah is made clear by confronting its aim and purpose with that of human law (*nimūs*). A law instituted by man aims exclusively at the best order in the State and removes injustice and oppression. As a result man obtains material happiness. But human law does not provide for the spiritual well-being—that is, the full development of the intellect so that man can reach his *summum bonum* in the knowledge and love of God. Nor is it concerned with man's opinions, be they right or wrong. On the other hand, a Torah comes from God and is intended to effect the best order of the body and the " faith " alike.[2] It is primarily concerned to spread the truth about God and the angels, to promote man's wisdom and understanding and to make him perceive all *Existing Things* in truth. Body and soul must be in right order. The soul is naturally superior to the body, but the body takes precedence in Nature and in time. Ultimate perfection and happiness depend on true leadership and good order of the community.

The true Torah is unique . . . there is no other and it is

---

[1] Crescas has greatly elaborated this idea in his *'Or 'Adonay*.

[2] Faith in contrast with body expresses clearly the God-centred purpose of the Divine Law and conceives of the intellectual perfection as a means to reasonable faith.

the Torah of our master Moses : it brings us the twofold perfection.[1]

Thus the Torah is raised high above any other law. How deeply Maimonides was impressed by the Greek intellectual virtue is evident from yet another quotation : *The Torah has given us the most important of the true ideas through which we reach ultimate perfection and called upon us to believe in them in general, viz. in the existence of God, His unity, knowledge, power, free will and eternity, which we can only understand after a careful study of other ideas. There are still other notions, belief in which is necessary for the best order of the State.*[2] That is to say, right beliefs are essential and indispensable if the perfect State is to exist. The Torah as the fruit of God's wisdom is the most efficient political constitution, for it secures the best possible administration and is the most perfect guide towards the establishment of right relations between men. But, if this were all, it would be distinct from the Greek *Nomos* only in degree but not in essence. Therefore its superiority derives from the fact that it leads man through the *mişwoth* to God, culminating in the *Imitatio Dei.*[3]

Maimonides' interpretation is in accordance with tradition in so far as it acknowledges the absolute authority and superiority of Torah. It is " Greek " in that it implies that the Torah receives its full realization in the political sphere. But here again we might point out that under the aspect of an

---

[1] *Morē*, III, ch. 27.

[2] *Ib.*, III, ch. 28. See also I, ch. 50, where Maimonides stresses against Yehudah Hal-lewi's sufficiency of faith without rational inquiry the necessity to supplement faith by knowledge of its truth.

[3] *Morē*, I, ch. 54. See also his *Eight Chapters*, ch. viii.

all-embracing " Law " the human community, organized in the State, is the natural scene of its realization.

It will now be clear that Messianism, the belief in the ideal ruler of the house of David who will rule the world *at the end of days*, not only forms one of the pillars of the Jewish faith but that it is, in fact, the realization of the Ideal State. In it the Torah rules once more supreme as foreshadowed by Isaiah : *For from Zion goes forth the Torah, and the word of God from Jerusalem.* Man can reach his goal only in the Messianic kingdom.

The most convincing evidence that Maimonides held that man can attain his end only within the Torah is that in his *Morē* III he explains the *miṣwoth* in substantially the same manner as in his *Mishneh Torah*. Any differences between them are due to the different purpose the author had in mind in writing each work, and to the different reader to whom each was addressed. The code was addressed to those who wished guidance for their lives as Jews within the all-embracing Torah. The *Morē* appealed to those in the first place who were perturbed by doubts whether philosophy did not run counter to Revelation. Thus, only the argumentation is different, for the basis is one in both, viz. the true Torah. The philosophical guide, the *Morē*, purported to show that philosophy teaches the same truth, but in a human and less perfect way. It showed at the same time that the application of philosophic principles and arguments and of scientific knowledge can bring to light what is hidden in the Torah.

It is mainly the latter point which has roused the critics. But Maimonides has only done what has always been considered quite legitimate in the

Halachic sphere, viz. to let the spirit prevail over the letter. His was an age of speculation when religious thinkers had to harmonize the traditional truth divinely revealed with the results of speculative reason. Therefore quite naturally emphasis was laid on knowledge and right opinions, but the ethical and practical side of the commandments was not neglected. The command, *Thou shalt love thy God with all thy heart*—the heart is the seat of understanding for a Hebrew—took precedence over all else. It could only be realized after man had come to deeper and deeper knowledge of the supreme object of his love, God. Such knowledge was impossible without the teaching of the Torah.

Some thought that this teaching alone was insufficient. It needed to be supplemented by the speculative sciences in the same way as the practical sciences helped to a better understanding of the practical precepts.[1] Others limited speculation and stressed practical, active piety in order to reach the same end. Others again put forward faith as the principal means by which man would reach his ultimate perfection and happiness.[2] But all agreed that knowledge was legitimate and essential. This could hardly be otherwise, for knowledge and understanding are as vital to Judaism as are justice and righteousness and repentance and forgiveness, so long as everything is related to God. But no thinker imagined the speculative sciences to be anything but a help towards a better understanding of the Torah.

This can best be seen in the attitude adopted by

[1] A fuller treatment must be reserved to the forthcoming study.
[2] See p. 204, n. 2.

Don Isaac Abravanel to Maimonides [1] in relation to speculation and rational interpretation of Scripture. Abravanel vindicates the miraculous character of prophecy against Maimonides' psychological interpretation of prophecy as a natural phenomenon by asking Yehudah Hal-lewi's question : Why were the great virtuous philosophers of Greece not prophets if prophecy was only a matter of moral and intellectual perfection ? But a rational interpretation often forced Maimonides to abandon the clear meaning of the text in order to bring out the identity of the Torah and Aristotle's metaphysics—with the notable exception of the *creatio ex nihilo* ! For Abravanel the Bible is clear in its own terms. Normally he is content with a literal interpretation. But where a literal interpretation seems to make no sense, he prefers an allegorical and figurative explanation. The real difference between them lies in the fact that while for Maimonides in metaphysics Aristotle has equal authority with the Torah, Abravanel always assigns to the Rabbis of old an authority higher than to Aristotle. But Abravanel was not averse to " secular " thought. He uses a philosophical argument if it can help to support tradition or to express more clearly the true meaning of the Bible in the thought-categories in use in his day. But it seems that he set less store on speculation than did Maimonides. He follows Maimonides whenever his views are compatible with tradition.

All Jewish mediæval thinkers meet ultimately on the ground of tradition in all questions affecting the

---

[1] For a fuller treatment than is here possible, see the present writer's " Don Isaac Abravanel, Financier, Statesman and Scholar," in *Bulletin of the John Rylands Library* (October 1937), pp. 445 ff., especially pp. 474 ff.

fundamental teaching of Judaism.   All assert, in
common with mediæval ideas, the essential unity of
faith and knowledge.   Nowhere can this be seen
better than in the contrast which they, especially
Maimonides, drew between the Divine Torah and the
Greek human law in its " political " aspect.   The
Greek theory of the Ideal State with its *Nomos* served
to make manifest to them that the Torah was the one
comprehensive " law," supreme above all others.

Short Bibliography

In addition to the sources and the literature quoted in the
lecture the reader may wish to consult the following books :

PARKES, J. : *The Jew in the Mediæval Community* (London, 1938).

Germania Judaica, ed. Elbogen—Freimann—Tykocinski (Breslau,
1934).

BAER, F. : *Die Juden im christlichen Spanien* (Erster Teil : 1. Band
(Berlin), 2. Band, 1936).

SHOHET, D. M. : *The Jewish Court in the Middle Ages* (New York,
1931).

GUTTMANN, JULIUS : *Die Philosophie des Judentums* (München,
1933).

STRAUSS, L. : *Philosophie und Gesetz* (Berlin, 1935).

IX

THE SCHOLASTIC ATTITUDE
TO THE LAW

BY

Fr. VINCENT McNABB

IX

Two quotations from St. Thomas Aquinas, the Prince of Scholastics, may fitly introduce what we shall say on the subject of our paper. Both quotations will be taken from that vast and unique synthesis of highest human thought, the *Summa Theologica*. To the question " Whether the New Law is distinct from the Old Law," he replies that they are different, not in species but in mode. In the course of his reply he says :

> " The New Law is not distinct from the Old Law, because they have both the same end, namely man's subjection to God ; and there is but one God of the New and of the Old Testament, according to Romans iii. 30. *It is one God that justifieth circumcision by faith and uncircumcision through faith.* . . . The unity of faith under both Testaments witnesses to the unity of end. . . . Yet faith had a different state in the Old and in the New Law, since what they believed as future, we believe as fact." [2]

The second quotation is taken from the answer St. Thomas gives to the question " Whether Christ conformed His conduct to the Law." He says :

---

[1] [The reader is referred to the author's treatment of the problem of law in his earlier essay on " St. Thomas Aquinas and Law " in *Blackfriars* (May 1929).—ED.]

[2] *Summa Theol.* (Eng. trans.), Parts i, ii, Qu. 107, Art. 1.

" Christ conformed His conduct in all things to the precepts of the Law. In token of this He wished to be circumcised ; for the circumcision is a kind of protestation of a man's purpose of keeping the law, according to Galatians v. 3, *I testify to every man circumcising himself that he is a debtor to do the whole law.*

" And Christ indeed wished to conform His conduct to the Law :—

" First to show His approval of the Old Law.

" Secondly, that by obeying the Law He might perfect it and bring it to an end in His own self so as to show that it was ordained to Him.

" Thirdly, to deprive the Jews of an excuse for slandering Him.

" Fourthly, in order to deliver man from subjection to the Law, according to Galatians iv. 4, 5.

" *God sent His Son . . . made under the Law, that He might redeem them who were under the Law.*" [1]

If an organism is what it will become, and if Scholasticism fruited in Aquinas, we can best study the relation of Scholasticism to the Law in Scholasticism's ultimate fruit, Aquinas ; and in such quotations as we have just read.

We are borne to this way of handling our subject by one personal and one impersonal motive. Though threescore years of life and some four-and-forty years of life in life's battle-front have left not a little time for philosophic study and thought, the present writer has always found in a page of Aquinas so much essential food for thought that to go further afield seemed a squandering of intelligence.

Moreover it was always the thought of Aquinas and never the history of that thought which seemed of greatest worth, and this not because it was what Aquinas thought but because it was true.

[1] *Summa Theol.* (Eng. trans.), Part iii, Qu. 40, Art. 4.

For this reason the very limitations of my years of study made it impossible to seek outside the vast philosophic synthesis of the Prince of Scholastics principles for dealing with the relations between Scholasticism and the Old Testament Law.

Yet even if this personal factor had not been imperative there would have been an impersonal factor that would have been imperative.

Almost hidden away in the *Summa Theologica*, at the end of the book on General Ethics and the principles of human acts, there is the great thinker's treatise on Law. It hardly contains more than eighty thousand to ninety thousand words. Yet it may be argued that, short as it is, it sets its writer at the head of the world's thinkers. It would seem to be the first great treatise ever written on Law. Assuredly it was the first treatise on Law which included in its sweep not merely the social arrangements made for managing road traffic or money-lending, but even the forces that make the sap mount in a blade of grass and those that make the stars keep their places in the vastness of the universe.

But for the writer of this paper, and indeed for any writer of such a paper as this, St. Thomas's treatise on Law could hardly be looked on as optional. This great treatise of the greatest of the Scholastics would give such a writer what he could find nowhere else in the thinkers who went before Aquinas ; and nowhere else more scientifically in those who came after. He would find what seems to have been the first and still seems to be the most scientific analysis of the Jewish Code of Laws—perhaps of any Code—that has been offered to the student of human institutions.

* * * * * *

From these introductory principles of approach to our subject we turn to the profound principles broached in the two introductory quotations.

The Scholastic as such was a Christian whose attitude to truth is summed up in Anselm's famous epigram : *Fides quaerens intellectum* (" Faith that seeks understanding "), whether it is the human faith that accepts human witness, or the almost greater faith that accepts the witness of the senses. The Scholastics, in search for fuller and fuller understanding, questioned what they heard and saw ; but, unlike the sceptics, they never questioned that they heard it and saw it.

When after thirteen centuries of Christianity these Scholastics turned their young fresh eager minds towards the Book of the Old Law and towards that faith in the unseen God which was the heroism of the heroes of the Book, they called it proudly *their* Book, because for them it was God's Book and God was their God. Carrying principles to conclusions, they proclaimed that the faith which moved Abraham to quit Haran, and moved the children of Abraham to leave the flesh-pots of Egypt, was moving their Western minds to follow Abraham and Moses, and still more to follow a Greater than Abraham and Moses out of the shadows of things visible into the realities of things invisible. Theirs was the same faith as that of Abraham and Moses. But whereas Abraham and Moses had a faith great enough to hold that Someone was coming, these Western children of Abraham and Moses had the greater faith which held that He had come.

For faith as great as theirs the Sacred Book, which enshrined what they called not merely the Law but

the Divine Law, became prized as no book ever was
or ever could be prized. The salvage of hand-written
copies of the Book left to us from monastic and
scholastic libraries still enrich the libraries of to-day.
All this felt and prized right to the Old and to the New
was due to the felt principle that, as in adding faith
to reason, so too in adding Jesus to Abraham and
Moses man's mind is not asked to give up but to grow
up, even though what comes of the growing up may
seem as different as the oak is different from the
acorn.

This attitude of reverence for the Old Law and
Testament was, if we may say so, raised to the infinite
by what the Scholastics felt, and the Prince of
Scholastics has expressed, in the words we have quoted
about the obedience given by Jesus Christ to the Law.
Scholastics were not of those who, from their merely
exegetical or merely social point of view, narrow Jesus
down to a religious or social revolutionary. To the
Scholastic, Jesus, far from being a revolutionary, was
hardly even a reformer. Neither they in their days,
nor we in our days, have a name to express His unique
function. He Himself has expressed it not as a sub-
stantive but as a verb : " Do not think I am come to
destroy the Law or the Prophets. I am not come to
destroy but to fulfil " (Matt. v. 17). His was the most
difficult of all religious or social functions, demanding
the fine art of " not breaking the bruised reed nor
quenching the smoking flax." When the divine gift
entrusted to Israel had to go out from Israel to the
world, there was needed that gentleness of omni-
potence which unfolds the bud to the blossom and
fulfils the blossom in the fruit.

As the Scholastics believed passionately that Jesus

was true Son of God as well as true Son of David, the Law which He fulfilled by obeying became sacrosanct to them.   Even the songs of Sion became their daily offering of official prayer to God.   With an instinct which carried on Israel's attitude towards God, they made it a daily duty to chant or say Israel's most characteristic psalm which begins : " Blessed are they that are perfect in the way, who walk in the Law of the Lord."

Had the people of God left us no other heirloom than this song of Sion on the nobility and divinity of Law, they would have given what no other nation has given to the world.   Perhaps this glorious song was first made for singing and first sung by some old priest-singer of the Temple, whose love of the Torah engaged his weakening memory with a device of verse.   Taking the letters of that alphabet which perhaps his own Hebrew people had first formed, he begins eight verses with each letter of the two-and-twenty ; and each of the verses is in praise or thanks for this people's beloved Torah.   His love for the law of his people has thus achieved something unique in literature ; perhaps unique in love.   But we should not have approached the study of Scholasticism and the Law if we forgot that this unique Hebrew song of praise, thanks, intercession, love of the Torah was the daily prayer of the Scholastics.

*   *   *   *   *   *

A further quotation from Aquinas will throw further light on the attitude of Scholastics to the Torah. Again it is taken from the treatise on Law.

" The Jewish people were chosen by God that the Christ might be born of them.   Consequently the entire state of that people had to be prophetic and figurative, as Augustine states.[1]

" For this reason even the judicial precepts that were given to this people were more figurative than those which were given to other nations. Thus, too, the wars and deeds of this people are expounded in the mystical sense ; but not the wars and deeds of the Assyrians and Romans, although the latter are more famous in the eyes of men." [2]

Did we not know whose words these were, the words themselves might suggest their Jewish authorship ; but could hardly suggest that their writer was a thirteenth-century Scholastic of Scholastics. The almost contemptuous reference to the Assyrian and Roman super-nations serves to show that the writer's measure of value is not the opinion of men but the judgment of God. Only a being's relation to the Absolute is that being's absolute relation.

If in showing the special relation of the Jewish nation to God St. Thomas mentions Assyria and Rome but not Greece, no doubt it was because Greece had never been one nation as the Jews, the Assyrians, and the Romans had been a nation. Greece had been less a nation or a people than a language, a speech, a thought, a Logos. But the word of Greek thought, glorious and world-victorious as it was, never reached the victory or the glory of " the Logos of Nazareth, and Word of the Cross."

The Western Scholastics, then, who looked upon Jesus the Son of David as being the very Son of God, went on to see in the laws of David's people not just the mould of a little self-conscious Eastern people, but the preparation for a coming of God Himself. This

[1] *Contra Faustum*, xxii. 24.
[2] *Summa Theol.*, Qu. 104, Art. 2, reply to 2nd obj.

view that a people and their laws were a long preparation for God's coming gave the Scholastics a higher conception of the people and of their laws than had yet entered into the minds of that people. The scandal of the Cross was that it was " Caritas nimia "—love too good to be true. But whether the Scholastics were right or wrong, they saw more in the people and the laws of the Old Testament than those people saw in themselves.

*　　*　　*　　*　　*　　*

Let us now turn to another quotation from the same treatise on Law :

" It belongs to the divine law to direct men to one another and to God. Now each of these belongs in the abstract to the dictates of the natural law, to which dictates the Moral precepts are to be referred.

" Yet each of them has to be determined by Divine or human law, because naturally known principles are universal, both in speculative and in practical matters. Accordingly, just as the determination of the universal principle about Divine worship is effected by the Ceremonial precepts, so the determination of the general precepts of that justice which is to be observed among men is effected by the Judicial precepts.

"We must therefore distinguish three kinds of precepts in the Old Law :—Moral precepts, which are dictated by the natural law ;

" Ceremonial precepts, which are determinations of the Divine worship ;

" Judicial precepts, which are determinations of the justice to be maintained among men.

" Wherefore the Apostle (Rom. vii. 12) after saying that *the Law is holy* adds that *the commandment is just and holy and good* ; just in respect of the judicial precepts ; holy with regard to the ceremonial precepts ; and good, i.e. conducive to virtue, as to the moral precepts." [1]

[1] *Summa Theol.*, Qu. 99, Art. 4.

1. In the almost mathematical simplicity and terseness of this fragment we have a characteristic example of Scholastic thought. Not everyone who reads it for the first time will realize that towards its platitudinous obviousness have gone centuries of thinking. For some years the present writer has sought to express his admiration for the marvellously obvious division of the Old Jewish Law by finding out the thinker who first broached the division. Not being an historian even in the history of philosophy or theology, I have consulted some of the European experts in the matter ; but all to no purpose ! I am therefore reduced to the necessity of supposing that here, as elsewhere, St. Thomas has not only robbed but enriched all his predecessors in thought.[1]

2. Students of primitive Christianity will perhaps

---

[1] [Maimonides in his *Morē Nᵉḇuchim* (III, ch. 26) divides the precepts into ceremonial precepts (*ḥuqqim*) not accessible to human reason, and judicial (*mishpaṭim*) within reach of human understanding. He includes, contrary to Aquinas, moral precepts in this second group. He would not have admitted that Moral Law and Natural Law are at one, as Natural Law is not accepted in Judaism (see Rosenthal, *above*, p. 200, n. 1). Cf. also Fr. McNabb's statement in his " St. Thomas Aquinas and Law," *loc. cit.*, p. 11 of offprint : " The blend of Aristotelian intellectualism and realism with Judaic revelation was a quality of Maimonides which St. Thomas, more than any Catholic thinker, might be expected to appreciate. To give praise where due, we must confess that had Moses Maimonides not written his famous book, *Guide of the Doubting* [*Morē Nᵉḇuchim*], there would never have been written a still more famous book, St. Thomas's treatise on Law." We may refer the reader to the monographs of Jakob Guttmann dealing with Maimonides' influence on Scholasticism and particularly on Aquinas : *Das Verhältnis des Thomas von Aquino zum Judentum und zur jüdischen Literatur* (Göttingen, 1891), especially p. 89 f., and *Die Scholastik des 13. Jahrhunderts in ihren Beziehungen zum Judentum und zur jüdischen Literatur* (Breslau, 1902).—Ed.]

be grateful for a division of the precepts of the Law which throws great light on the first internal, and almost fatal, misunderstanding that might have wrecked the Church of the Apostles. Between what are so often called the Judeo-Christians, with James as leader, and the Gentile-Christians, with Paul as leader, there had come the question whether the Law should, or should not, be abrogated. We have but to read St. Paul's Epistle to the Galatian Churches and St. Luke's account of the Council of Jerusalem in the Acts of the Apostles to realize how this inevitable question of what the Christ had or had not abrogated in the Old Law came near destroying the Christian Church's most essential quality, its unity. The source of this misunderstanding, as of so many tragic misunderstandings, was in an ambiguous use of words. Between the party of James and the party of Paul the dispute was carried on with the largely ambiguous words " Works, Law, Faith." There was no clear definition of what was meant by Works and what was meant by Faith. Above all, there was no clear verbal distinction as thirteen centuries later there was a clear distinction between three different groups of precepts in the Law.

The Law contained self-evident principles of the Natural Law in the form of a Decalogue. These Moral principles, as St. Paul would have agreed, could not be abrogated by Christ.

The Law also contained Ceremonial precepts. These, being essentially figurative of the Messiah and His work, had necessarily to be abrogated by being fulfilled.

Lastly, the Law contained certain Judicial or Social precepts destined to organize a people socially. These precepts, being neither fundamental nor figurative, might be changed to meet changing circumstances.

It is quite clear that a claim to abrogate the Law without mentioning what precepts of the Law it was claimed to abrogate, might lead headlong Christians to deny indispensable principles of the Moral Law. The later forms of Antinomianism justified these fears. No wonder, then, that James, after fully accepting the authoritative ruling of Peter, called the attention of the Council to the fact that there were certain natural Moral precepts, such as the precept against fornication, which the Council must not even seem to abrogate.

In other words, when James agreed that circumcision should cease to be obligatory but asked the Council to declare that fornication should not cease to be forbidden, he was implicitly distinguishing between Ceremonial precepts which should be abrogated and Moral precepts which should not and could not be abrogated. This distinction, which was implicit and not explicit in the amendment moved by James, was explicitly formulated some thirteen centuries later by the observant, accurate mind of the Scholastics.

It is, then, a matter of no little interest that this distinction latent in James's words needed some thirteen centuries before the Scholastic mind took it from its latent and implicit state to one that was at once patent and explicit.

James's grave concern to safeguard the immovable Moral precepts on which all law should be based, is not without its significance in days when States, having occupied the throne of God, claim to be the one Absolute in the sphere of Politics and Morals.

The apologists and apostles of these States make either an explicit or implicit claim to rest their polity on the principle : " That is moral which is good for the State."

Another quotation may serve to supplement what previous quotations have led us to say. Replying to the question whether the precepts of the Decalogue are dispensable, St. Thomas says :

> " Precepts admit of dispensation when there occurs a particular case in which if the letter of the law be observed the intention of the law-giver is frustrated.
>
> " Now the intention of every law-giver is directed *first* and chiefly to the common good, and *secondly* to the order of justice and virtue whereby the common good is preserved and attained.
>
> " If therefore there be any precepts which contain the very preservation of the common good, or the very order of justice and virtue, such precepts contain the intention of the law-giver and are therefore indispensable. For instance, if in some community a law were enacted such as this—that no man should work for the destruction of the commonwealth, or betray the State to its enemies, or that no man should do anything unjust or evil, such precepts would not admit of dispensation.
>
> " But if other precepts were enacted subordinate to the above and determining certain modes of procedure, these latter precepts would admit of dispensation in so far as the omission of these precepts in certain cases would not be prejudicial to the former precepts which contain the intention of the law-giver. For instance, if, in the safeguarding of the commonwealth, it were enacted that from each ward some men should keep watch in case of siege, some might be dispensed from this on account of some greater utility.
>
> " Now the precepts of the Decalogue contain the very intention of the law-giver who is God.
>
> " For the precepts of the first title which direct us to God contain the very order to the common good which

is God :—while the precepts of the second table contain
the order of justice to be observed among men, that
nothing undue be done to anyone, and that each one
be given his due ; for it is in this sense that we are to
take the precepts of the Decalogue.

"Consequently the precepts of the Decalogue admit
of no dispensation whatever." [1]

In making this profound analysis of the fundamental
moral teaching of the Jewish Torah, and making it
with a thoroughness beyond any Jewish teacher,
St. Thomas was setting the little people of Palestine
not only beyond the Assyrians and the Romans but
even beyond the Greeks. From past ages Greece had
received no forms of literature or philosophy that it
had not passed on to future ages enriched and adorned.
Yet it never enriched mankind in the sphere of human
action as Israel enriched mankind by giving them the
Decalogue. Plato in his *Republic*, and Plato's pupil
Aristotle in his *Ethics*, have given a moral synthesis of
man, individual or collective, in the four virtues of
Prudence, Justice, Fortitude and Temperance. But
in admitting this achievement, perhaps this greatest
and anonymous achievement of Grecian genius, two
facts must not be forgotten. First, the moral Absolute
which demanded and measured these four virtues
was not an absolute. It was only that stage-absolute
the so-called State ; which in idea should be the State
or Commonwealth itself, but in reality is usually a
person or a group of persons who have imposed their
will on the wills of the people.

But the Jewish moral synthesis was a complete
outline, giving room for all the necessary fulfilling in-
lines. It was not the people who were the Absolute ;

[1] *Summa Theol.*, Qu. 100, Art. 8.

and whose moral perfection consisted in some worthless self-expression or some baseless relation to itself. For Israel the Absolute was not Israel but the God of Israel. Their fundamental Law uttered itself, as if with thunder, in the opening words : " I am the Lord thy God that brought thee out of the land of Egypt and out of the house of bondage! Thou shalt not have strange Gods before Me." Israel's God was—God.

This first difference between the Jewish Moral Law and the moral writings of the Greeks was accentuated by a second. Even the greatest of the Greek moral teachers have left us classical moral treatises. On the other hand, Israel has left us not a moral treatise but its Code of Moral Laws. The Greece of Plato and Aristotle, if it had wished to have philosopher kings, had men of sufficient skill in scientific ethics to have given Hellas an immortal Code of Laws. But Israel did what Greece did not do, and Rome did not do, and Egypt did not do, and no country but Israel ever did.

At least, such was the opinion of Aquinas, the Prince of Scholastics. As his was the genius which gave to the ethical thought of Plato and Aristotle what day gives to dawn, his opinion on the Torah is of weight.

Under the guidance of this great, patient, humble searcher after truth in what many headlong historians would have called the debris of the Pentateuch we find the romance of a world-wide religious, and therefore social, beginning. A handful of foreign work-slaves, threatened with the destruction of their family life, choose to come out of what we should call a high civilization. They are led by a fellow-Hebrew of liberal education who has found the appeal to the sword futile. With inner vision he leads the handful of his fellow-Hebrews into what they themselves call " the desert." In what we might call socially their " nascent state," they promulgate a Moral Code as the immovable basis of their polity. No other people, even the most intellectual, ever did what was done by this group of escaped work-slaves. Then some thirty centuries afterwards, in the most intellectual centre the world of scholars had ever seen, this Code of Moral Laws is found to be a complete and accurate grouping of the Natural Moral Law. Moreover, its precepts are in strict scientific series, showing that they came not merely from an upright conscience but also from a clear and well-furnished mind.

Two incidents seem to express something of what the present writer felt as St. Thomas unveiled for him the profound moral doctrine of the Jewish Decalogue. One day some walk-fellows of Tennyson, noticing that he was no longer with them, went back and found him on his knees, his hands in a little runlet of clear water that crossed the road. Quite unaware of their presence he kept saying : " What a poet is God ! What a poet is God ! "

A few years ago one of our foremost astronomers and mathematicians, after measuring the universe (with or without Einstein's relative and therefore unreliable measure), is reported to have said : " The maker of the Universe is a Mathematician."

St. Thomas by showing me, as a great thinker alone could show me, the scientific deeps of this Code of a little shepherd people made me say : " The framer of this Law has intelligence on the level of genius."

* * * * * *

One last and longest quotation from the Prince of Scholastics will bring authentic witness to the scientific reverence given to the Jewish Law by the Scholastics. The vast unwieldy bulk of social laws embodied in the Torah is reduced by St. Thomas to manageable and intelligible size under four simple essential headings :

1. Laws regarding the Rulers.
2. Laws regarding the Ruled.
3. Laws regarding Foreigners.
4. Laws regarding Families.

In answer to his own question : " Whether the Judicial precepts were suitably framed with regard to the relations of one man with another "—he writes :

" As Augustine says (*De Civ. Dei*, ii. 21), quoting Tully, *a nation is a body of men united together by consent to the law and by community of welfare.* Consequently it is of the essence of a nation that the mutual relations of the citizens be ordered by just laws.

" Now the relations of one man to another are twofold : *some* are effected under the guidance of those in authority ; *others* are effected by the will of private individuals. And since whatever is subject to the power of an individual can be disposed of according to his will, hence it is that the decision of matters between one man and another—and the punishment of evil-doers —depend on the direction of those in authority to whom men submit. On the other hand the power of private persons is exercised over the things they possess ; and consequently their dealings with one another as regards such things depend on their own will, for instance in buying, selling, giving and so forth. Now the Law provided sufficiently in respect of each of these relations between one man and another.

" For it established Judges, as is clearly indicated (Deut. xvi. 18) : *Thou shalt appoint judges and magistrates in all thy gates . . . that they may judge the people with just judgment.*

" It also directed the manner of pronouncing just judgments according to Deut. i. 16, 17 : *Judge that which is just whether he be one of your own country or a stranger : there shall be no difference of persons.*

" It also removed an occasion of pronouncing unjust judgments, by forbidding judges to accept bribes (Exod. xxiii. 8 ; Deut. xvi. 19).

" It prescribed the number of witnesses : viz. two or three.

" And it appointed certain punishments to certain crimes.

*   *   *   *   *   *

" But with regard to possessions it is a very good thing, says the Philosopher (*Polit.*, ii. 2), that the things possessed should be distinct, and that the use thereof should be partly common, and partly granted to others by the will of the possessors. These three points were provided for by the Law.

" Because, in the first place, the possessions themselves were divided among individuals ; for it is written (Num. xxxiii. 53, 54) *I have given you the land for a possession, and you shall divide it among you by lot.*

" And since many States have been ruined through want of regulations in the matter of possessions, as the Philosopher observes (*Polit.*, ii. 6), therefore the Law provided a threefold remedy against the irregularity of possessions. The first was that they should be divided equally ; wherefore it is written (Num. xxxiii. 54) *To the more you shall give a larger part, and to the fewer, a lesser.* A second remedy was that possessions could not be alienated for ever ; but after a certain lapse of time should return to their former owner, so as to avoid confusion of possessions. The third remedy aimed at the removal of this confusion and provided that the dead should be succeeded by their next of kin ; in the first place, the son ; secondly, the daughter ; thirdly, the brother ; fourthly, the father's brother ; fifthly, any other next of kin.

" Furthermore in order to preserve the distinction of

property, the Law enacted that heiresses should marry within their own tribe, as recorded in Num. xxxvi. 6.

" Secondly, the Law commanded that in some respects, the use of things should belong to all in common—Firstly as regards the care of them, for it was prescribed (Deut. xxii. 1–4) *Thou shalt not pass by if thou seest thy brother's ox or his sheep go astray ; but thou shalt bring them back to thy brother.* Secondly, as regards fruits. For all alike were allowed on entering a vineyard to eat of the fruit, but not to take any away. And especially with regard to the poor, it was prescribed that the forgotten sheaves, and the bunches of grapes and fruit should be left for them (Lev. xix. 9 ; Deut. xxiv. 19). Moreover whatever grew in the seventh year was common property as stated in Exod. xxiii. 11 ; Lev. xxv. 4.

" Thirdly, the law recognised the transference of goods by the owner.

" There was a purely gratuitous transfer. Thus it is written (Deut. xiv. 28, 29) : *The third day thou shalt separate another tithe . . . and the Levite . . . and the stranger and the fatherless and the widow shall come and shall eat and shall be filled.*

" And there was a transfer for a consideration ; for instance, by selling and buying, by letting out and hiring, by loan and also by deposit ; concerning all of which we find that the Law made ample provision.

" Consequently it is clear that the Old Law provided sufficiently concerning the mutual relations of one man with another." [1]

*　　*　　*　　*　　*　　*

When it is realized that the genius who has condensed so much social doctrine into so narrow a space has also, in a style of equal condensation, added fivefold to this analysis, it will be agreed that Scholastics have not acted ungenerously towards the Jewish Law.

[1] *Summa Theol.*, Qu. 105, Art. 2.

But students of legal institutions and functions may be struck by the contrast between this analysis of a definite Code of Laws and the classification of Roman Law made by the Byzantine jurists of the time of Justinian. The division of Roman Laws into laws concerning Persons and laws concerning Things was hardly more than a convenient mode of card-indexing the vast mass of statutory enactments which for the moment defended and in the end helped to overwhelm the Byzantine Emperors. A modern English jurist has summed up the limitations of these Byzantine jurists who did their best to make the Corpus Juris Civilis into something more than a dead corpse.

> " The first sections of the Institutes of Gaius and Justinian attempt an explanation of the most general ideas of Law. The effort was to a large extent frustrated by the weakness of the Roman Jurists in the Philosophy of Law, and the defect of their technical language." [1]

In other words, these case-lawyers to whom was committed the duty of tidying up the accumulated litter of Roman enactments and decisions found their time so fully occupied with the task of tidying that they had no time for finding out principles not so much of tidying the law but of making the law. Their acquaintance with psychology and ethics—the very bases of Law—was of the slenderest, because Rhetoric rather than Philosophy offered them the chance of a successful legal career.

But when the Prince of Scholastics, in the last years of his life, began to find order in the Book of Laws which he revered as the Book of God, he brought to the task a fullness of all that the Byzantine jurists

[1] *Roman Law*, by William A. Hunter (London, 1876), p. xxxvii.

lacked.   Plato and Aristotle had given him that sound
psychology without which no mind is really safe in
ethics or even in history.   To the Greek thinkers,
again, he owed that scientific synthesis of ethics
which alone could guarantee an accurate view of the
most important section of ethics, viz. Law.   Hardly
within the limits of one lecture could we express all
that is meant by saying that St. Thomas finds the
unifying principle in Jewish Law in Justice, both
general and particular.   Aristotle had largely been
his teacher in this matter of general and particular
justice.   But Aristotle had too dim a notion of God
and too clear a notion of the State (which to him was
not Greece but Alexander the Great) to be a complete
master of his Christian pupil.   A Greater than
Aristotle or Aristotle's pupil had taken His place
amongst the little people who called Abraham their
father on earth and God their Father in heaven.   The
Word had become flesh to dwell and die amongst
men.   The Absolute had served His creatures by His
life and death.

Though this profound reverence for the God-guided
laws of the God-chosen people is in every line
Aquinas wrote about the Torah, reverence never
overawes him into disuse of his powers of observation.
Even with the help of all that modern critics find in
the works of previous commentators the critics will
find few or none of the essential laws of Jewry that
have escaped St. Thomas's attention.   More than in
any other of his works does he give us something fuller
than a very accurate outline, the first need for accurate
thought.   But within this outline, he has offered us
not a few of the essential in-lines of such patient
accuracy that the jurists and statesmen of the

twentieth century, in accepting what he offers, may well feel grateful to the Scholastics of the thirteenth. Acute observation is seen in such minute matters as the number of witnesses psychologically necessary for finding out the truth—or again in settling the difference between paying a workman's wage and a tradesman's bill—in the quality of persons exempt from military service—in the steps taken to make public opinion discover a murderer—in the causes justifying the death penalty—in the difference between selling town houses or country houses—and in many other matters of minute social detail. But all these matters of seemingly trivial detail in the Social laws examined by St. Thomas are examined and classified, as we have said, by the fundamental principle of general and particular justice. It is in this sense that we venture to claim that, at the hands of the Prince of Scholastics, the laws of Israel have received not *a* codification but *their* codification. The order he finds in these laws is not accidental but essential to the laws themselves.

With the broaching of this view of St. Thomas's commentary on the Torah we may be allowed to pass on to a personal conviction. If I call it personal it is only that my hearers may take it for what it is worth, and that they may realize how little it is worth, as the speaker's personal conviction. Yet some acquaintance with the Book and the genius who comments on the laws in the Book, and moreover some experience of life in life's battle-front, daily deepen a conviction of mine which I can only confusedly express.

In the same Book which offers to our mind a Code of Laws, shown by genius to be the work of collective genius, we are told the story of how this little people, despising their littleness, wished for kings, and that God gave them kings in His wrath. Under a like stirring of ambition or avarice the modern world is everywhere athirst for what is great : but great in width or bulk. Little people tend to become or to be absorbed in super-nations ; and super-nations tend to demand and produce supermen whose " might is right," and, to use a word of a master of words, whose law is " sword-law." For the present writer the great thing in contrast with the little thing is of little social worth. Only the little things, only the little nations, will have survival value. Genius, whether political or economic, must now set to work upon fostering the little self-supporting units ; the little self-sufficient communities of men. But if statesmen ever come to see the need of fostering little units of self-sufficiency, they may be expected to see in the laws of a little people what was seen by the genius of Aquinas—viz. a Code of Nature's own laws for man as man ; and for collective man as collective man.

To conclude : When St. Thomas set about finding order in the tangle of Jewish Social Law, General Justice became not merely, as to the Greeks, a relation of man to the community as an Absolute but a relation to God the Absolute. Moreover, Particular Justice became not merely a relation of equality between man and his fellow-man but their relation of love to God who equally loved them both. In that love of God for both, they were both brothers. And in that love of God for all, authenticated on Calvary, mankind was, or was made to be, a Brotherhood of Man.

It is surely significant that this great city and the

mother school of this great city should be minded to discuss the Law of the little God-guided people in these days of such needed guidance. More than at any recorded time of history do we hear the words and feel the hot desiring breath for " the Brotherhood of Man." If this city gave its name to a school of economic *laissez-faire* now fruiting in world-wide class-war, these lectures on the great moral, religious and social laws of a little Eastern people may be that city's inspiring return to ways of wisdom and peace. That return would be all the more speedy and inspiring if the words you have allowed me to speak to-day beckoned us to the thought of that great—perhaps greatest !—genius of the West who has left us such a monument of his reverence for the one great Law Code of the East because he found in it the God-given laws that perfect Man as Man.

AFTERWORD

THE Epilogue comes after the fall of the curtain, when nothing can be added to the drama that has already ended ; the function of the epilogue is thus neither to augment nor to criticise, but merely to sum up the impressions of the spectator. The series of lectures is finished and the purpose of this brief afterword is really to congratulate the editor and his colleagues on the achievement of their task, " to propose a vote of thanks to the Chair," in fact.

This volume, the third of the series, differs somewhat in scope from the two that preceded it. They were marking out the ground for the camp : now the first tent has been pitched. Here a definite problem has been set to each lecturer : his limits, though wide, are yet fixed. Consequently, there is a clear purpose to be observed throughout this book : a note of continuity is visible from the first page to the last. It is remarkable how one chapter picks up the thread precisely where the previous one left it : there is no break of thought, no re-adjustment necessary. One would have imagined that this result was due to skilful planning and much collaboration and interchange of drafts. Of planning and care on the part of the editor there has, it is obvious, been much. But the book has grown naturally and no meetings, I understand, have been held between the various lecturers. Yet the book makes a harmonious whole.

This is to a large extent due to the unity of outlook of the lecturers. " The evolution of law for man . . . is a particular case of revelation," says Professor J. Murphy (p. 25), and Dr. Fish concludes with the words " the promulgation of laws by political authority (was) . . . in a real sense (a) religious act." Dr. Wheeler Robinson reiterates the same idea for early Israel in his treatment of the terms *Torah— Nomos—Lex*, and Professor Robertson shows how the Samaritans, without the aid of prophets and psalmists, succeeded in finding ethics in the Pentateuchal Code, which in itself is such a wonderful combination of law and morality. Then Dr. Travers Herford takes up the tale and deals with the union of law and religion in Pharisaism. He is followed by Professor Manson who, in spite of certain reservations, has much in common with him : for he holds that Jesus did not reject the Law or disregard its commands lightly ; he reserved the right to criticize freely and break through its restrictions. Now this, in principle, is pure Pharisaism. For Ps. cxix. 126 was interpreted as : " It is time to work for the Lord, hence they have made void Thy Law," in other words, for the sake of religion, the Law may sometimes be set aside. The difference is not one of principle but of degree, though it may certainly be remarked that sometimes the extent of the degree almost justifies the use of another term.

Professor Gibb shows how, in Islam " Law was a part of the Science of religious duties," and Dr. Rosenthal traces this further in mediæval Judaism. The concluding lecture, of Fr. Vincent McNabb, drives home the argument in regard to Scholasticism and answers some of Professor Manson's reservations.

Thus we see an underlying unity in the book

and for this Dr. Rosenthal's editorial work must be commended : his own lecture is a skilful compression of scholarship, most attractively offered to the reader.

These brilliant lectures are an admirable example of the success which can attend the composite treatment of a difficult problem. In this fine work scholars of all shades of belief have been represented, and the inclusion of two distinguished Roman Catholics has repaired a deficiency in the two former volumes. Such an undertaking makes not only for scholarship but for peace and love ; it is a powerful demonstration, a demonstration badly needed to-day in the face of disruptive agencies like Fascism and Bolshevism, of the force inherent in learning, freedom and brotherhood to establish truth and goodwill. The combination of teachers of these different denominations in this task will produce far-reaching results. *Scripta manent* : the book, published under the excellent auspices of the S.P.C.K., will penetrate into many scattered churches, synagogues, colleges, and, it is to be hoped, homes. Thus it will influence wide circles and will spread the Spirit of God over many distant fields.

May this volume be the forerunner of others. London, Cambridge and Manchester have done their share : it is for other centres of learning to take up the torch.

H. LOEWE.

August 15, 1938.

I. GENERAL INDEX

II. PASSAGES CITED

E. Koran

SŪRA xxxviii. 43...160 ; xlv. 17...
147 ; xlix. 10...147

F. Mishnah

Baba Kamma viii, 1...104
Pirke Aboth i, 15...195

G. Babylonian Talmud

Joma 84b...105
Succah 20a...93
B. Bathra 12a...110, 174 ; 60b...175
Sanhedrin 21b...93

H. Josephus

Cont. Apion. i. 209–211...130

Printed in England at THE BALLANTYNE PRESS
SPOTTISWOODE, BALLANTYNE & CO. LTD.
Colchester, London & Eton